CONTENTS

LIFE'S A GAS!

The Memoirs of a Gas Engineer

by

Spike

This book is dedicated

To

Martin Bartlett

My D.S.O. (District Service Officer, and friend too) who helped 'mould' me into the gasman I am today, if it weren't for your guidance, knowledge, and understanding, I would never have led such an 'interesting' life.

Thank you so much for believing in me, and giving me the best opportunity that many others never had.

You were, and still are a true gentleman.

I wish you the best in life, as you truly deserve it.

Therefore, please DO NOT read on (I know you will).

Acknowledgements

Not forgetting of course, the men and women who worked at 'Witney Depot', for the sake (and sanity) of the engineers and depot clerks, I will mention no 'real' names, just merely use your 'nicknames' or change them slightly, to which anyone else reading this will be clueless.

To every one of you, you are a moment in my life that helped me become a gasman, for this I am forever grateful, it's been an amazing, funny, yet sometimes tearful time (mainly of laughter, yet some of sorrow).

However, you will always be so very dear to me.

Also, to the ones we have lost along the way, you will be forever in our hearts and in our minds.

Jimmy – D.S.O.

'Chad' – Gas Engineer

'ACE' – Gas Engineer

'Dickie' – Gas Engineer

Nashmeister, the years we spent together working (not as chutney ferrets) will always remain as some of the funniest times in my life, if I miss anything from my 'Old Shire', it's working with you, I love you like a brother.

Pablo and Ian, great times, great laughs, and never forgotten, love you dearly.

Simon Rees the Welshman, a loveable rogue.

To my fellow apprentices, friends and family, who have had to listen to my 'adventures/drivel' throughout the years, Pierre, Dickie, Jez & Lynn, especially my dearest of friends Dave Lamb, who has probably heard more than any other, yet has still remained, and always will be 'my brother from another mother'.

To Guy Tipton, my friend from the start of Woodgreen secondary school (1S) in 1983, how the years have ticked by. I would never have thought that technology, by the wonders of Facebook, that I would be back in contact with you in 2021, and playing your amazing album 'These Days' through to the finish of my book in 2023.

This has kept me company on the many evenings I have spent compiling this book, thank you for creating such a great album, you truly are a talented man, and a lifelong friend.

I ask whoever reads this to purchase this amazing album, you won't be disappointed.

To Lisa, my beautiful girlfriend, my best friend, my soul mate. Thank you for your support through possibly the rockiest times of my entire life. It's because of you that I've once again found love, something I never thought I would find again.

To Zoro, the crazy little dog, that stole both our hearts. The unconditional love, and laughter you give is what make our little family complete…Love you Tank.

To Murley, a 'long-lost-life-long-friend', who is capable of chatting sense and changing to waffling utter guff at the flip of a coin. Your knowledge as an engineer is the best of anyone I have ever met, and working with you was always great. The laughs we have will continue for as long as we have air in our lungs my dear friend.

Onwards Brown Bottle!

Finally, to my mum who watched me hatch, and my two sisters who have stood by me, despite being a right pain in the arse, especially when I carried out the 'grand eyelid opening of the church bells'.

(Possibly my third book… 'A boy called Wiff').

And of course, the general public who more often than not, were unwittingly involved in my 'high jinks'. Your names will be changed to protect you, although you were never in any danger, whereas I was…. usually because of you!

So be grateful I've not 'grassed you up', and you're not serving a 2-year stretch with 'Jimmy the Squealer' passing the soap in the showers.

Apologies if I've missed anyone, but 35 years of working with:

CH_4 (Methane/Natural Gas)

CO_2 (Carbon Dioxide)

CO (Carbon Monoxide)

H_2O (Water)

Has made me 'slip a few cogs' in the gear department.

Finally, to Mack…

" We know why we're so unhappy, so why don't you just…shut up fatty!"

PROLOGUE

FREE

Now I have your attention, this book is a mere 'grain in the cat litter tray' of my working life as an 'industry trained' and 'highly skilled' gas engineer, from a 'green behind the ears' school leaver, to a 50 plus year old man (half a century…how did that happen?), who still loves his job…yes, I really do.

All of the episodes you are about to read are true, yet not recorded on any form of paper, or electronic device, merely plucked from my 'child genius' mind as I recall them, and chose to write them before I 'lose my marbles' and encouraged by Dave Lamb (thanks mate), with the hope that you my dear reader, will smile, maybe even chuckle at what you are about to read…

May you all be truly thankful. Amen.

I am eternally grateful for the fact there was primitive technology, and no social media in those days.

I hope this book takes a dedicated spot on a shelf in your WC, and if it doesn't interest you, at least you have an emergency toilet roll.

You can place it next to the second 'emergency toilet roll' of a book, which is my three years as an apprentice at a college in Oxford (in progress).

ONE FINAL, YET VERY IMPORTANT NOTE…

This book is written about my working life from 1988 to 1998 (possibly further years to follow), those times were very different in society from this year (2023). If you feel that you might be offended by this then I suggest you place this book back on the 'BEST SELLER' shelf in EVERY bookshop in the land, or, by the toilet…otherwise read on.

I'm not going to apologise to anyone, this is my account of my life in this period of my history, it can't be changed. To the ones included in this book, they're made of true mettle, and actually won't give a toss.

I hope you enjoy reading this book, as much as I have writing it, bringing back so many memories. I've reduced the number of memories of each Engineer, so as to keep it from being a cure for insomnia.

A very tiny spoiler…Ever been electrocuted by an old lady?

Read on.

GOLDEN RULE

Safeguard Life – Safeguard Property.

CHAPTER ONE

Independence Day – 4th July 1988

At 8 o'clock on a glorious sunny summer morning I arrived at Witney Depot. A stick thin school leaver with the typical 'council house boy' haircut, a mop of blonde hair, almost touching my shoulders, but trimmed out of level on the fringe due to me fidgeting as my mum approached with the carpet scissors (love you mum).

I was in my immaculate BG issued uniform, comprising of a sky-blue collared shirt, navy blue work jacket, and trousers to match, with steel toe capped shoes that would allow me to hoof a football for at least a mile!

A sea of blue and white vans confronted me covering the car park, with the single storey depot protruding like a solitary red brick lighthouse in the background, the sun's rays bouncing from its mustard-coloured metal roof, like a beacon of hope.

I walked in to be met with a flurry of activity, my hands felt clammy, my heart rate similar to that of a hamster that had spent all night on its wheel. To my left a mass of men in matching yet differing shades of blue uniform similar to mine, they were shuffling paper work and chatting amongst themselves (it was almost as if the 'sea of blue' had broken through the windows and continued its destruction inside).

They were stood at waist height, white and blue speckled laminate worktops, with a single wooden blue painted locker beneath, there were six in line, and 3 rows back-to-back. The surrounding walls were mainly a shade of Magnolia, with notice boards scattered around covered with BG propaganda posters. The ceilings were made up of 'asbestos free' ceiling tiles with numerous lights strategically placed to ensure not one area would be dark (not the case for the store area).

At the end of each set of lockers was a lowered worktop of similar colour, with a chair, and an odd looking tv, 'Technicians' sat here, these were men I aspired to be in my latter years of my apprenticeship, in the meantime, I was a mere 'tadpole' in this rock pool.

To my right, a more serene environment, a waterfall of calm, yet busy in movement, a carpeted area, with an array of light oak desks, pot plants, and comfortable blue padded office chairs where numerous people were sat.

There was a woman in my foreground, the Depot Clerk, wearing a pink coloured blouse, with beautiful auburn hair. She was surrounded by a desk making her out to be in my 'mind's eye' a mermaid perched amongst some rocks, although she didn't have a starfish in her hair.

She was typing on a computer whilst talking on a telephone (to this day I still can't manage this, as many of my male friends too, it's a skill that only women have of multi-tasking, if a man claims he can, then he's a liar.... or a woman! Don't get me started on the magic of these 'wondrous human beings' able to watch a film, chat, and do 'Facebook' nowadays, as that surely be 'witchcraft'?).

However, she went from 'Mermaid' to 'Siren' very quickly by any man who dare cross her, to which he was firmly put in his place (quite incredible how 'Steph' cowered at her voice, yet in a blink of an eye could crush your skull in his left hand...that being his weak hand).

In the background were three men in suits, each sat behind individual desks, their description will follow.

I decided to park myself at the end of the first row of lockers on an empty Technician's desktop, with the hope that someone would spot me, and introduce me to my life in the 'big wide world of work, not school'.

After a few minutes there was movement, but not from the 'pool of tranquillity' on my right, but my left, one of the engineers had broken away from the tempest.

He strolled towards me, a brown flower-patterned mug in his hand, clasped like a precious family heirloom, he had the build of a giant 'wombat', quite short but sturdy, a tattoo on each arm, a receding hair line, and his main feature was his impressive pair of eyebrows and moustache, almost like an 'hypnotic set of furry caterpillars'.

"Alright boy, I'm Mickle, I have coffee with two sugars" he said.

Roll back 6 months...

School careers teacher "If anyone asks you to make a cup of tea or coffee you say "no, I'm not here to do that, I'm here to learn".

Roll forward 6 months...present day

My schoolboy brain kicks in and repeats those same words "No, I'm not here to do that, I'm here to learn" .... (Stop the time for a few seconds...this comment would seal my fate for a while) Mickle stands there for a few seconds, then his 'caterpillars' begin to dance... "oh really?" he replies, then turns and shouts "Steph!".

I chuckle in my mind thinking "what sort of a 'fairy' is he going to be with a name like Steph!?", before I get chance to think to the end of this sentence, a man the size of a very large 'blue planet destroying asteroid' appears, he eclipses the sun's rays as he enters 'our orbit' and my mind empties of all childlike humour as Mickle explains in what feels like hours in slow motion, my 'rebel like' attitude, but in seconds...

If you can picture this, it's the best example I can give you of Stef's first grip...

You're at the amusement arcades, you put money in the crane/grab/claw machine to get a furry monkey prize, you spend a small fortune, but win nothing...

This is actually NOTHING like it!

Stef grabs my hair successfully first time, and manoeuvres me in 'one fell swoop' to the kitchen, his voice deep and grumbly, almost like the 'bass' level in a nightclub that's a bit too loud, makes my chest vibrate as he says "Get your f*cking hair cut boy" tugging my 'golden locks' then moves to my shoulder, he squeezes gently (in his mind maybe, but to me, it's numbed the left side of my body like a 'Vulcan death grip' executed by Spok from Star Wars*), and brings me within view of 4 large metal kettles boiling on the gas rings of a cooker. He points, then produces a blue mug from one of the cupboards.

Steph had a blue mug, black coffee, no sugar.

Mickle had a brown flowery mug, white coffee, two sugars.

I won't bore you with the other selections, but 35 years later I still remember the cups and contents of the depot staff. However, 'darker clouds' were forming as other engineers had 'clocked' my arrogance, and they too were going to put me in my rightful place...at the bottom of the food chain.

The only way to break this curse would be the following year, when Mickle asked me to join him at the lockers (a real privilege to join the ranks, only as a fledgling mind you), and to watch a repeat of my transition from school to work with the same act on 3 new apprentices, and him bellowing "STEPH!", the same look of humour on their innocent faces, then terror, as the 'sky blue behemoth' walked into view.

My day continued with less trauma, after making a **LOT** of Tea & Coffee, I met my District Service Officer (DSO) Martin Bartlett (MB), a tall clean-shaven man, donning a very smart charcoal coloured suit, white shirt, and a perfect 'Windsor knot' tie to match his suit, his shoes were highly polished and dark, to match his hair and bespectacled eyes (no they weren't highly polished, just dark). He had an astonishingly deep voice, to the point where it completely threw me, it was actually deeper than Steph's, yet not so loud, therefore I had no fear of natural defibrillation when he spoke.

After introducing himself and the role within the company, he then spent a considerable amount of time running over my daily menial duties of tea & coffee making, scouring the car park for screws or nails to prevent punctures, sweeping the yard and the stores, cleaning around the skips, along with the 'Do's and the Don'ts' of working for BG, however, he kept it simple, as he could see at this point...

I clearly was.

The other man sat next to Martin was Jim, he was of similar build, but with a lot more years under his belt, he wore a much more aged suit, grey hair that looked similar to 'a bundle of steel wool', small darting eyes, a rather large nose and chin to match, dare I say it, and no malice meant, a lifelike version of Mr. Punch (of Punch & Judy seaside fame). Along with a pipe stuck in his 'chops', creating an array of cloud around him almost like his own atmosphere.

The third man was from a separate department of BG, yet he was stationed at our depot, he was 'Gimpy', he was the manager of the 'Distribution' side. Here's a little insight into how the gas networks were managed...

Distribution - Pipelines in the road and up to the gas meter were dealt with by the 'Distribution' department gangs, these were tough men, they would dig down (usually with a 'fag in their chops') through anything to get to a gas pipe, whether it was to install new, replace, or repair it. Come rain or shine, these were the human equivalent of a badger... 'fearless, hard as f*ck, but partial to a cup of tea and biscuits from Mrs. Gimlet if offered'.

Service - Gas meters, pipework and appliances in the house were dealt with by the 'Service' department, service engineers, clean uniform (usually) and a vast array of knowledge and skills to service, maintain or replace anything that burned Natural Gas in the home.

-

After my initial introduction to the staff, I turned to see a number of engineers watching me, almost like children studying an ant under a magnifying glass, before the death ray of the sun atomised it. Two engineers in particular were edging towards me, at a slow pace, one looked like the 'Honey Monster' of similar build and a wild beard to match, the other a short, but stout man sporting a 70's porn star moustache, with a glint of mischief in his eye. These were 'Turv' & 'Wedge', their first words to me were "get ready for you initiation boy" to which they cackled maniacally and left, leaving me perplexed, and somewhat worried too.

Martin decided I should go with the most senior engineer Dick Ford; his experience and life skills were the perfect start that I needed on my road to becoming a gas engineer. We left the comfort and safety of the depot, and I followed Dick to his van, we rounded the corner to be confronted with a blue and white LDV Sherpa van with sliding doors, I use the term 'van' loosely, as that too had seen many years of service for British Gas.

I climbed in the passenger side after heaving on the door to open it, once inside I heaved the door shut and fastened my seat belt. Dick however, climbed in, sparked a fag up, reversed out of the parking bay, driving some 10 miles to our first port of call with his door open, and no seat belt on, clanging one fag after another.

The conversation was limited; however, I always remember one thing he told me, that was "you'll have a job for life my boy, you'll be taxed and you'll die", he wasn't wrong, but to a 16-year-old boy it made no sense.

I was with Dick for my first week, his 'rapport' with everyone around him was amazing, he would captivate a room, customers would listen to his wise words (usually tips on how to prevent them from blowing themselves up). I felt honoured to have spent time with this man, he was what I feel many of the other engineers aspired to be like (and to be honest, they did).

It wouldn't be long before I was introduced to the other engineers, I'm not religious, but so God help me!

*Spok was in Star Trek

CHAPTER TWO
Becoming 'Spike'

Following on from my initial 'hair pulling' from Steph, I decided that I would take his advice, and made my way to a barber shop that weekend. I was informed by my mate 'Kev' that we had to be there by 7:30am, otherwise our hair might be different as Alf liked to get on the Whiskey by 8!

I met Kev, and to our delight we were the only two in the 'salon', this was in fact more like a room of a house, with worn lino as the flooring, and wallpaper to match, a large window with net curtains only permitting the sun's rays to enter.

Two barbers' chairs, and a mirror fixed horizontally above a shelf containing the tools of his trade, both, the length of the wall. A few pictures of men with 1960's hairstyles donned one wall, on the opposite was shelves with 'Brylcreem', shaving cream, and boxes of prophylactics, or in those days known as 'rubber jonnies'.

Alf appeared from behind a curtain, a grey-haired man, with a 'bombardier's moustache' that was finely waxed at the ends to form a point, his small dark brown eyes were protected by a grey thicket of eyebrow. He was dressed in a grey jacket (similar to what you would see a foreman in a factory wearing), slacks, and a huge pair of brown leather shoes, sorry, I meant canoes...they were enormous! He would never go over in a gale that's for sure.

He cast his beady eyes at us both, and asked what style we wanted, Kev said "usual please Alf, and same for him", he turned raised his monobrow, and walked over to the sign at the door, as he flipped it to 'closed' he said "won't have time for anymore after dealing with that mop my boy".

Kev was done in no time, slipped Alf a fiver and bid farewell, wishing us both good luck. I sat in the chair, and was soon mesmerised by how skilled Alf was, the bones in his fingers, were moulded into the scissor handles, yet the majority of the time he used the clippers, he also used a 'giant afro' comb with a spirit level on it, this was to shape my hair into a 'flat top'. The man was a master of his trade.

For what seemed like an eternity, Alf finally hung up the clippers, put the scissors in a jar on the side, opened a cupboard door revealing a large bottle of Whiskey and a glass, he filled it to the brim, and proceeded to 'chug it down' like it was his last, he filled it again, but before he could continue his session, I interrupted him by asking "how much do I owe you?".

"A fiver" came the swift reply, as he began to guzzle. I didn't think this was adequate considering the amount of time he had spent 'shearing' me, so I purchased a tub of hair gel, and gave him £10 and told him to keep the change. I left as he was half way through his third tipple, waving goodbye without looking as I left. (I visited Alf every two weeks for five years, until sadly he retired. What a truly wonderful man).

I got on my bike and began to pedal, only to be met with a strange whistling noise, I stopped, it stopped, I started pedalling, it started again. I inspected my brakes and wheels for maybe a slight buckle, nothing.

It was only when I turned my head to look across the road that the whistling stopped, and returned when I was looking forward, the 'penny dropped', it was the wind whistling through my gold hoop 'pirate style' earrings that adorned my lug holes (yes, that was fashionable in the late 1980's – 90's), as they were now 'open to the elements' after going from a 'mini haystack' to short back and sides (grade 1).

I arrived at the depot Monday morning to be greeted by the

whoops and clapping from the engineers, along with 'yes sir sgt. Major sir' and other military comments that I'll refrain from mentioning.

Sporting my new haircut, along with half a tube of hair gel to ensure it kept its shape (I later learnt to only use a 'thumbnail' of the stuff) I was the main attraction that morning as I made the tea and coffee, having engineers walk into the kitchen to collect their beverage, and have a feel of the 'natural spikey safety hat'.

From that day onwards I would be known as 'Spike'. Although still a sprog, I felt part of the gang.

35 years later, a select few still call me this, which causes confusion to the unknowing, as I now shave my head completely, there are sadly no 'spikes' to see.

CHAPTER THREE
Engineer Role Call

Witney depot as per 1988, consisted of 23 gas service engineers, three of which were 'Technicians' (the 'elite').

To this day I have the utmost respect for the engineers that helped (and sometimes unwittingly) trained me, each had their different 'skill sets' which made up an 'efficient and well-oiled machine' that was part of British Gas Southern (one of the divisions of this once great company).

The Technicians were no exception to this, yet they were one step ahead in their knowledge base. Some may have different opinions on this, however, it's me writing the book and not them, to me, they're my heroes.

A couple of months into my apprenticeship, and thanks to Martin Bartlett (MB), I had ventured out into the 'big wide world' with the majority of these, learning some good things, but also, some not so good things. My mind didn't take long to be converted from school boy to young man, not so much a 'baptism of fire'...

But at 'Gas Mark 4' for 3 years.

Here are the Engineers, some will not have much of a story to their name, this isn't out of disrespect, or that they were boring (trust me, as life has sped by, I realised NONE of them were), it's just that I only spent a small amount of time with them.

The list isn't in alphabetic order, but in layout of the depot lockers in my memory.

CHAPTER FOUR

Beetle

Shop Steward/union rep – a 'rotund' bearded fellow, who looked like (the legend of Swap Shop) Noel Edmonds in a convex mirror, donning a hearing aid as an addition.

Whilst working with Beetle (using that term loosely), we would spend hours in the depot whilst he was carrying out 'Shop Steward' duties. Leave the depot mid-morning to do a boiler service in the morning, then spend several hours at his house, while I played football with his son, he slept in his chair after a 'hearty lunch'. We would then do a boiler service in the afternoon and then he would drop me off home.

I remember one job in particular that didn't take his fancy, this was to service a gas boiler in a village hall. He had pre-written an N.A. card (No Access) whilst sat in the van, he then 'tip-toed' up to the front door of the village hall like a Ninja assassin, and used the 'sponge door knock' technique^.

This wasn't a code word for a grotesque murder of a target, this is where the engineer arrives at the door, and clenches their hand into a fist and pretends to knock the door, but at the last second hovers their knuckles a 'gnats knacker' distance from the door, thus, fooling any would be onlooker that's a bit of a 'curtain twitcher' into thinking that they're trying their best to gain access to the property.

And despite his numerous ailments that prevented him from carrying out the majority of work required as a gas engineer, he was very nimble on his feet, his running speed could've given an athlete a cause for concern.

How do I know this you may ask? Well, this wasn't down to me witnessing this with my own eyes, but the security camera footage sent to our depot by the village hall secretary. BG had written a rather stern letter advising them that unless they gained access to the hall, the warranty on their boiler would be void.

After contesting that it was impossible that there was nobody at the hall that day (or the previous two missed appointments by the same engineer) due to the fact there was 30 people having a yoga class, with all windows and doors open to help ventilate the hall. The secretary was seething about this letter, and sent in video footage, catching Beetle red handed. He was reprimanded, and the job was completed first time by another engineer.

This was a gradual 'stepping stone' into the pool of employment, but one that I would soon be looking at as more of a 'skimming' stone, to not look back on again as any form of training, and this style of work practice wasn't for me.

I only worked with Beetle for a week, then Martin moved me onto someone who wasn't suffering from 'workshyness'.

However, I am guilty of this a few years later in Milton Keynes. It was a very rough estate, if you parked for too long, your wheels were gone.

I was on a nationwide gas meter exchange programme, as most of us were after the servicing schedule had been done, where any meters with an 'S' on them needed to be changed.

I needed to change a gas meter at this certain property, I could see through the door, a male and female were on the sofa, they were naked, and from my memory, they weren't wrestling.

At this point, I introduced the sponge door knock technique^, and prevented the 'silver back' from dismounting his mate, and tearing my limbs off.

CHAPTER FIVE
Chad

(R.I.P.) – I'll never speak ill of the dead, it's disrespectful, and there's certainly no need for me to do so with Chad, or anyone else who sadly departed this earth way too soon.

Chad was a tall man, average build, with light brown hair that was styled to the liking of a person who had 'found electricity' by touching a pylon with a kite.

Now the next part would fit perfectly into a Dickens novel...he liked to smoke fags (of the normal variety); his van (carriage) ashtray would have put any 'house fire remnants' to shame. he also liked his beer...along with playing pool, and darts.

My first experience with Chad, was to assist in installing new iron 'carcass' pipework to a building site (Court Gardens a cul de sac, off Judds Close, Witney) in the midst of Winter, this was my first experience of working in sub-zero temperatures for eight hours, I hated it, and still do.

After loading up the van with numerous fittings, we ventured out of the depot, the wind was bitterly cold, we got in the van, and whilst I was blowing into my hands, and before we reached the main gate to the yard, a fag was lit, and a fresh carton of milk had been opened (if any of you remember the 'cartons', there was a knack to opening them without getting soaked, Chad could open this with one hand, whilst driving, and smoking).

We arrived at the site, snow on the ground, along with 'Jack Frost' biting at all extremities, the builders were nowhere to be seen...

"can't lay bricks with frozen muck" sprang to mind from a previous overheard conversation.

I unloaded the fittings, as Chad brushed the snow from the iron pipes that were in frozen bundles, he grabbed a hammer and walked over to an upturned oil drum, that was usually used for the builders as their water supply for their cement. He broke the 3 inches of ice, dropped the hammer, and slipped his hands into the water without even a flinch of an eyelid.

"Here you go boy, warm your hands" as he swished his hands around like he was washing up, and searching for the final tea spoon. I gazed in horror, being a paperboy from 12 to 15 years old, I knew the pain of Winter (I hate it to this day), but my hands were nearly numb, and I trusted my mentor. I dipped my hands in, the pain was excruciating, as Chad grinned at me.

"It burns my boy, but gets better", he handed me a rag, he wasn't wrong, as I lifted my hands out, and dried them. I could feel warmth running into all of my once frozen digits, wriggling them, he handed me some suede work gloves, all was resolved.

I surveyed the surroundings, the building site consisted of a few bungalows and houses, all of which had rooves, but no windows or doors, just bare skeletons, hence the name 'carcassing'. Chad measured up the length of pipe, cut it with a large hacksaw in what seemed like seconds, then used a manual threading machine 'Stock & Dye' set to thread the pipe.

He could sense I was in some stage of Hypothermia, so handed the gauntlet to me, to measure, cut and thread the next set of pipes whilst under the gaze of his bloodshot eyes. It only took a few cuts of pipe using the hacksaw, and threading those pipes and I was sweating my 9 ½ stone body weight in what felt like minutes, at one point peeling off my jacket as I was too hot.

Chad was a tough bloke, cold never affected him, it might have been due to the fact his blood alcohol content was 'a tad out of kilter', to the point where he was a walking de-icer can, infact, at one stage he was living in a garage (whilst awaiting to move into his flat), and I recall him asking for a can of de-icer, not for his van windscreen, but for his tv screen.

I've never experienced the extreme temperatures since those days, going from 'bastard freezing' to 'boiling alive' in a short space of time. I think I could've qualified as an Astronaut after that, but that was an 'easy job', nothing compared to 'carcassing' with Chad.

CHAPTER SIX

Mossy

A tall slim man, with dark hair, and a mischievous glint in his eye. He was the depot comedian, great at giving customers some 'top tips' on the usage of their gas appliances, one in particular sticks in my mind.

I was with Mickle on this occasion (a few months into my apprenticeship), we called at a property to service the boiler, the customer opened the door Mr.'G', and we all ventured into his kitchen where the boiler was.

As we prepped the area with dust sheet, 'Henry' (the vacuum... Ok Murley?) being plugged in, and tool roll unravelled, 'G' asked "you two fancy a cuppa? we both replied "yes please" (a golden rule was to always accept a cuppa as you never knew when you'd get another, this didn't apply if the house you entered, the dust sheet was used to protect your tools and knees, not the carpet, or the kitchen could only be entered after using a flamethrower).

We then watched 'G' place the kettle onto the gas hob, then walk up to the edge of the rug, taking his time to have his feet set in a certain angle, he then leaned across an 'imaginary' gap with the stature of a rugby player in a scrum of 'invisible men' and lit the gas ring to which the kettle was sat on.

I glanced at Mickle, he was looking as confused as me, I could tell this, as his 'face furniture' was performing a tiny dance.

As the beverages were served up, Mickle enquired "What's with the leaning over to light the hob, have you done your back in?"

'G' replied "Oh no, I'm fine, we had one of your engineers out a few weeks ago to look at the ignition on the hob, and he said the only way it would work was if I stood like that, a Mr. Moss I believe?".

Mickle knew that this was a trick by Mossy and was in no way true, sadly the timing wasn't to Mickle's advantage…or mine, he'd taken a mouthful of tea at the point 'G' had confessed. Mickle unable to hold down the eruption of laughter that was about to ensue had two options:

i)   Keep his mouth shut, inhale the tea into his lungs, and possibly drown, eyes bugging like a Chihuahua on LSD, and his face furniture finally meeting together to see his demise.

ii)   Spray the entire contents of his mouth over his apprentice's back, as the apprentice was occupied servicing the boiler.

Just in case you hadn't guessed it, it was the latter option.

As I was drying my back with a rag from the tool roll, Mickle was explaining to 'G' that he had a very rare 'allergy to some teas' which brought about this reaction, he offered his deepest apologies, and would make the required adjustments to the hob to save 'G's' back, 'G' nodded and left us to it.

As I finished off the service, Mickle did nothing to the hob as there was nothing wrong to put right, and just watched me, whilst emptying the plate of biscuits, and chortling to himself.

Once complete, Mickle beckoned 'G' into the room who was completely oblivious, and on our departing thanked Mickle for his alteration to the hob which meant his rug could be moved, and he no longer had to perform the 'Praying Mantis' Yoga position.

The next day Mickle asked mossy about it, it turned out he had been called to a 'faulty ignition' on the gas hob, he'd fixed it, but 'G' was a 'repeat offender' of complaining about the engineers so he could get a discount on his 3* service contract, even though he never really had a problem, and was always nice to their faces.

Therefore, Mossy thought it be only fair that 'G' deserved some 'harmless payback'. It worked; 'G' never called up again to complain.

CHAPTER SEVEN
Winky

A blonde-haired chap, who was of average height, he'd been 'built up' through three years of being trained to the 'highest standards', he had the physique to show that he was a bloke that you knew could look after himself in a 'bar brawl'.

He had been 'released into the wild' after qualifying at college, and being assessed 'on the job'...sorry, I'll reword that...being assessed 'out on the district' in a customer's house (with their approval of course, they wouldn't just arrive and terrify the 85-year-old occupant).

Winky was the trainee of Ace, he spent the majority of his apprenticeship with Ace, therefore his mannerisms, his appearance, were all of a similar ilk.

This never wavered, even in the most difficult of times, when time was **NOT** your friend, especially when you had to get to the Witney Depot 'Christmas Do' at 19:00 hrs, and so the story goes...

08:00 - Winky was given me to assist him in fitting a gas 'wall heater' in a chapel in a village called Freeland, the survey had been done (by M.B.), the materials had been delivered to the depot, the van was loaded, we were all set.

09:00 - We arrived at the afore mentioned chapel with 'gusto', the 'wind in our sails', I set about laying dust sheets down, preparing the tools, drills and the ever faithful 'Henry' vacuum (Ok Murley?), as Winky surveyed the workplace, all seemed straight forward (understand this, after 35 years of being in the industry 'straight forward' is nonsense, it will curse your job, and this was no exception here).

09:30 - We unpacked the wall heater, and used the paper template to mark the wall for the flue, once marked, we began to drill using a new piece of technology of its time, a 'diamond tipped' core drill (I'll give you an example of what this drill bit is capable of... the channel tunnel used a Tunnel Boring Machine (T.B.M.), this was a smaller version) This amazing bit of kit consisted of a bar that connected the drill to a metal cylinder with 'diamond tipped teeth' fixed at the tip, in the centre it held a 'pilot' drill to keep it centralised on the initial drilling, this then had to be removed after the initial 'core hole' had been formed. It also came with 'extension bars' to allow it to defeat the thickest of walls.

10:00 - The drilling began, Winky taking the lead role, Henry's nozzle taped to the wall to extract the dust. After 20 minutes of continual drilling Winky was sweating like 'a person wanting to fart in a lift', yet the drill had driven into the stonework just a few inches, as he mopped his brow.

I took over, and began drilling, the drill itself weighed a fair bit, but the force of the drill bit revolving was a force to be reckoned with, this was to be proved when my 16-year-old arms couldn't match the 'torque' when the drill hit a bit of rough stone, I spun round in a complete circle like a gymnast, as the drill 'bit' into the stone, I released my grip, and regained my posture from the 'stunned chimp' that I was on the floor. Winky was clearly shaken by this (being a 'kind hearted soul') and insisted that I just "watch the expert".

12:00 – Winky & Henry needed a break, we sat and ate our sandwiches, me in my pristine uniform, and Winky looking like he had been in the Sahara in the midst of a sandstorm.

12:30 – Drilling started again.

13:30 – Drilling stopped.

13:35 – Winky made the executive decision that the core set was as much use as a 'chocolate fireguard', so we would use the 'old fashioned' way of doing things, the drill and core set was packed away.

13:45 – We started to chisel the stonework away with a lump hammer, chisel, and bolster, we took it in turns to penetrate the wall.

15:00 – Partial wall collapse.... fear not, we're not talking life threatening, only that from a 5" hole that was required to poke the heater 'flue pipe' through, we now had a hole that would have allowed short parishioners to leap through.

Little did we know that the 18th century chapel builders were 'cheats and bodgers' of their time, they'd built the chapel with stone work, yet the cavity of the walls was a mass of loose stones (we found out later that this was the 'norm' for building at the time, so I retract my comment, you weren't 'cheats and bodgers'), once we had removed two larger stones inside, the rest just fell apart.

At one-point Winky was sweating more than 'a fat kid in a sweet shop' as the innards of the chapel prolapsed, and we only had two bags of 'B.G. ready mix' on the van (B.G. Ready mix, was a ready-made mortar mix that was grey, it came in 5kg polythene bags. It was 'a shade of grey' that matched <u>NOTHING</u> that we 'made good' with, even GREY bricks and mortar didn't match the 'B.G. ready mix grey'.

If you ever spot an unsightly boiler/fire/space heater flue through a wall when you buy/rent a place.... yes, it was a professionally industry trained gas engineer that did the 'making good' with that NON matching mortar).

16:00 – The wall heater was on the wall, and the task of 'backfilling' quarter of the chapel's stonework was a daunting task, which we accomplished with grit, determination, two bags of B.G. ready mix, some soil from the surrounding rose beds, and a few jugs of 'holy water'.

17:45 –

Gas supply checked for leaks – check!

Gas heater tested – check!

Work place clean and tidy, Chapel secure – check!

Winky driving like he was 'possessed' so we could get to the 'Christmas Do' – check!

Scottish person walking past with a pair of lovely patterned trousers – check!

18:15 – We arrived at my house, Winky mounting the kerb at an awkward angle and at speed like a trainee stunt man, following through with this temporary title by blowing the rubber tyre off the metal wheel, thus disabling his chariot.

18:20 – Winky had now transformed into a 'one-man F1 pit crew', waving me on to go and get ready, he had the old warped wheel off, and the spare one on in a matter of minutes…he went from being in my sister's year at school - ok, to gas engineer – better…to this – the man was a legend!

19:00 – We arrived at the Christmas do separately, but we danced like brothers that night on the disco dance floor.

CHAPTER EIGHT

Stef

A dark-haired chap, the largest gas engineer in our depot, with the grip of a 'Terminator' (an Arnold Schwarzenegger film), the strength of ten men, a 'walking wall of muscle'.

You've read about my introduction to this 'man mountain', here's the rest.

Stef would take great delight in 'hugging' engineers who were caught unawares, he was like a Boa Constrictor, once in his grip, you would succumb to his 'deep grumbly chortle' as part of your body went numb. I saw one engineer who had been caught, squeal, and he actually 'clicked' as Stef's grip took hold, he walked like a crab for a couple of days after, until Stef straightened him out after another squeeze.

He also enjoyed tightening up any gas, and water connections to the point where the metal warped slightly, and any other engineers working on it in the future would burst blood vessels attempting to undo them for servicing needs…one thing that was sure of is that the gas joints would never leak…they were too scared to.

I used to try and avoid going with him for the above reasons, but also, he would never let me do anything, not even carry his tool roll. For this additional reason I would hide in other engineers' vans, under a dust sheet, and hear his 'siren' call "Spike…. Spike", then fade away, I knew I was safe, and would wait for the engineer to drive away from the depot before revealing my whereabouts by shouting "It's Spike, I didn't want to be with Stef!".

The first couple of times was a 'touch cloth' scenario for all involved, as my young mind didn't think that it would scare the living daylights out of a man driving a 1 tonne van, thinking he was on his own, and nearly ended in my 'victim' engineer nearly crashing the van!

Despite his behemoth demeanour, and knuckle dragging manner, he had a heart of gold, always willing to help anyone, more often to show off his brute strength, to which many engineers had caught wind of this, and used it to their advantage.

He helped one of the engineers move house to save on a removal company, they hired a van. Stef moved the majority of the furniture on his own, insisting the engineer would be in the way. At one point he walked out of the back of the hire van with a washing machine under one arm, and a tumble dryer under the other (how true this is I'm unsure, but I'll never question it, let it be in the 'sands of time' that this happened).

I remember M.B. advising me in my final year of my apprenticeship that I needed to pass my driving test as I would be driving a van, if I successfully passed my final exams. I had 13 driving lessons, and thankfully passed my driving test first time.

Stef escorted me around the local garages, and I spotted the car of my dreams a 'V' reg MK1 VW Golf, I got the car with a discount and an 'extended' warranty after he 'sealed the deal' for me at no extra cost. I was forever grateful, and signed the paperwork, as he gently shook the car dealers' hand for some considerable time, no doubt stopping his pulse on the left side of his body.

Stef was a force to be reckoned with…FACT.

CHAPTER NINE
Mickle

As you may recall, Mickle was the first engineer to introduce himself on my first day, little was I to know that many an adventure lay ahead for me in his company, sometimes a bit 'awkward', but mainly fun packed. Thanks Mickle.

An average sized bloke with incredible 'performing face furniture', his eyebrows and 70's porn star moustache were something to behold, especially when he was asking questions to a disgruntled customer, they were almost hypnotised by the 'triangle of hair' (which it formed when he raised his eyebrows) and usually ended up agreeing to whatever Mickle had suggested.

Mickle was a good engineer, despite what other people may have thought. Ok, he was a 'wind up' merchant, but he wasn't lazy, he was an intelligent bloke (this only came to fruition from me deciding to write this book, and the 'penny dropped' a long time ago), he allowed me to carry out the work using his tools, whilst supervising from a distance. He had the confidence to teach me, as well as ensure I was safe, along with capturing the confidence of any customer.

This is exactly how I have trained every apprentice/work experience person that has been with me, allowing them to get their 'hands dirty' using tools to fix, and sometimes make mistakes too. But be there to put it right, and support them, show them how to put it right.

That my friends, is how I believe we all learn things correctly, sometimes, it doesn't go according to plan, hence the reason for this book.

We work with water, we're going to get wet, we work with gas, we're going to get burnt. But if we do it right, it won't hurt us. That's why we do it right.

There are a few stories to say the least, however, this one will forever stay in my mind.

Mickle was very fond of two tabloid newspapers...'The Sun', and 'The Sport' (neither of which appealed to me at an age of 16...I was an innocent young man) these were mainly full of topless women, made up stories that were so 'far-fetched' they were more fantasy than reality. Along with hundreds of adverts for 'Adult chat' lines charged at £1 a minute, and 'local masseurs' (without sounding like a grandad, £1 in 1989 was a fortune.... Considering, you could have taken your entire family on holiday a few years later for that very same price thanks to 'The Sun' if you collected the tokens... great).

On this one particular day we were working in Witney. In the morning, servicing boilers, then off to Kidlington for an afternoon of the same thing.

Our lunch hour arrived, we grabbed a couple of portions of chips from 'The Penguin' fish & Chip shop, situated on the Burwell estate, and ventured back to the depot (If you ever get chance to visit my old Shire, please visit this place, as there is nowhere else in Oxfordshire that you will ever enjoy such a feast).

There were a few engineers with the same mindset, all in different stages of 'stuffing their faces' (not to be confused with 'stuffing their faeces' which is what my pc tried to 'auto correct' as I typed this, that's a different arena/past time/lunch break), as Mickle ate, he perused the Sports back pages, and almost spat his food out, as he spotted a 'local masseur' that was actually local...infact... Kidlington!

His excitement was of a level that nowadays a police constable would have 'tasered' him, and he would've been gnawing on his own leg. However, this wasn't the case as it was 1989, and he beckoned me over, as the other engineer's ears 'pricked up' (surely that should be one word…'enginears'?). I tried to interpret Mickle's words, but his excitement was reaching a euphoric level, I stepped in and asked "what are you on about?".

I gleaned from his hand signals that he'd found the previously mentioned 'masseur', and we needed to make a phone call to arrange a meeting…my apologies, did I say 'we'? What I actually meant was 'me/I'.

What I want you all to know is that Mickle was single at this particular time in his life, and that I was never 'press ganged' into the actions that I carried out, I think it was a growing, wanting of acceptance, almost a primitive 'pack' mentality in my young mind, I also want you all to understand we weren't all perverts.

I made my way over to one of the depot phones, ensuring I added the prefix of '141' before I dialled the rest of the number to 'Mandy's Magical Massage'…it started to ring… I put the phone on loud speaker for the audience to hear…a few moments later I heard the voice of Mandy say "Hello"

Without a pause I said "Oh good afternoon is that, Mandy?"

She replied "yes, how can I help?"

Me:" Could I please book myself in for a massage?"

Mandy: "Yes of course, when would you like?"

I turned to Mickle for a date/time, whilst in the background the other engineers had abandoned anything they were doing and were captivated by the 'hot date' that was about to be made.

Mickle broke the silence by whispering "This afternoon, ok?"

I echoed his request down the mouth piece of the phone, Mandy replied "oooh I could squeeze you in at 2:30pm, that ok?"

Mickle gave the 'double thumbs up', and the time was agreed.

Before I continue this, I want to reiterate to you all that this to me, was a step into being accepted as part of the family, not of perverts (because they certainly were not that) but to be part of the camaraderie, and belong to these hard, funny, and highly skilled group of men.

Back to the story...

We drove to Kidlington, a warm sunny summers day, listening to 'The Scorpions - wind of change' playing in the background on 'Atlantic 252 LW' on the radio, whilst we both discussed the plan of carrying out a 'recce' of the road/property/woman that Mickle was potentially going to have this 'Magical Massage' with.

As the plan was finalised, we arrived at our destination as planned - 2:00pm, we would use our highly skilled and trained minds, along with a Telegan to carry out investigative work to trace and repair a suspected gas leak, this was a guise for Mickle to decide whether he would visit Mandy in his own time.

One thing that should be brought into question is the use of the Telegan (and not our highly skilled and trained minds), as this piece of equipment only detected the products of combustion from a boiler flue, and not a gas leak of any kind.

We jumped out of the van, like excited school kids on a trip to Hill End Camp (highly recommended, near Farmoor), gathered our highly sensitive testing equipment to carry out the façade of tracing the reported gas escape at number 39.

With me being the 'door knocker', I knocked on the first door number 25, as the gent answered, I asked if they had smelt gas or reported anything, to which he replied 'No'.

This pattern continued until I reached the 'goal' of number 39, I was a bundle of nerves, in a fight or flight mode I knocked the door. Mickle by this time was continually prodding the analyser tube into the path, gathering imaginary readings into an imaginary 'Gasco seeker' (the correct piece of equipment for leak detection).

The front door was of solid timber construction, giving me no idea of what I was about to witness. It opened to reveal a rather large lady, with dark shoulder length curly hair, donning a semi-transparent dressing gown (she was infact so large she could have had her own 'postcode'), she had bright red lipstick, and piercing blue eyes that were fixed upon me like a laser designator, she looked suspiciously at me, then Mickle, and then said "Hello, how can I help you?"

My mind was racing, I could feel myself glowing with embarrassment, I felt like a naughty school boy being questioned by a teacher, then that very rare moment my grey matter kicked in, and I enquired nervously...

"Good afternoon, have you reported a smell of gas?", her pursed red lips became unpursed as she replied "no", and slammed the door shut.

I scuttled up the path, and met Mickle, we then both continued to 'scuttle' back to the van like a pair of migrating crabs, we clambered in the van and drove off to our next legitimate customer.

The journey was silent, Mickle, as far as I know, never saw Mandy again.

CHAPTER TEN

Slim

Slim was the brother to Stef, you would never have believed it, and would probably still wouldn't that these two are related if you saw them both in the same room, and especially if you spoke to them both.

Although slim wasn't of the same build to his older sibling, never be fooled by the strength of a man by his size, slim had the same strength, he just chose to aim his 'powers' to the greater good, rather than the dark side.

Slim, like Stef, had a 5 o'clock shadow at 8:05am, he was shorter than Stef, and carried a bit more weight about his midriff, he had dark curly hair that was immaculate (I later realised why, as his wife was a hairdresser, so he had literally just stepped out of a salon every morning), aside his beautiful locks he donned a pair of gold hoop earrings, that would have made him a perfect extra in a Pirate film, especially with our country bumpkin accents.

I have a few varied memories of Slim, one is that whilst carrying out work, especially of a complex nature, his tongue would venture out of his mouth, almost like a python protruding from its lair after sensing its possible next meal venturing nearby. As an apprentice, more often than not if we were servicing boilers all day, after the same 4th boiler, I would actually find watching Slim's tongue more entertaining to watch than the boiler service.

The other memory that springs to mind is this one...

BG had won a tender for the installation of central heating systems in what were to be luxury apartments, in a huge conversion project of a mill in Chipping Norton, the place was called 'Bliss Tweed Mill'. Situated in a valley surrounded by lush green pastures, a picture postcard idyllic setting in the Cotswolds (in 1989 they were being sold at £1m each, these were definitely luxury).

A manager was brought in to 'manage' this enormous amount of work, never seen before by the engineers at Witney Depot, this would be 'all hands to the pumps' to complete the work in the timeline that the developers had given BG, with a nasty little sting in the tail called a penalty clause, meaning if we didn't complete the work in the allotted time, then it would start costing BG money, and that wasn't going to happen.

The manager was a man simply known as A.R. his infamous saying was "I'm so bloody busy me, aye", he was a portly middle-aged Yorkshire man, smartly dressed in a grey suit, white shirt, and grey tie to match, as my memory recalls he was 'dripping' in gold, with a gold bracelet, and numerous gold rings on his fingers, similar to a seedy second hand 'Arthur Daley' type car salesman (target audience right there kids) of a similar era.

A.R. liked to smoke cigarettes, so much so, that his grey 'Teddy Boy' quiff hairstyle had a golden-brown nicotine stain through the front of it, but only in the place where a fag was permanently positioned in his mouth.

Smoking was the fashion in those days, infact everyone seemed to smoke! I have to say it was 'normal' tobacco, I don't want anyone to think we were all off our noggins on weed! You could smoke on the top deck of a bus, in cinemas, with 'ashtrays' built into the seats of both afore mentioned places.

You could smoke in pubs, although restaurants were laughable, you had a 'smoking' and 'non-smoking' area in the same room, it was just divided by a 6ft partition, so the smoke drifted over (I didn't succumb to this habit until I was 19, not through BG I'd like to add, but from the group of mates I knocked about with at the time).

My deepest apologies for my digression, let us return to the rolling hills of the Cotswolds...

On a bright, sunny, yet very frosty November morning, as a pheasant scuttled and screeched amongst the frozen foliage, the serenity was broken as the sound of a fleet of blue & white diesel BG lorries were winding their way down to the mill, they lay to rest beside huge blue shipping containers. As a young apprentice, the sight was breath-taking, this showed the prowess of a huge company, which made my heart beat faster with pride to be part of such a wondrous entity.

The materials were unloaded from the fleet into the containers, like a colony of blue ants, the vast number of BG staff were an amazing regimented order and soon made short work of this task.

Slim was part of a two man install team, there were three teams, along with 'yours truly' to ferry tools, materials, cups of coffee, tea and sandwich requests from the van down the road.

I carried out my tasks to the very best of my abilities, despite the sub-zero conditions, I never felt cold, as I had to scale the numerous levels via flights of unlit stairs to each floor. The lifts were still on the plans, yet not installed, a poster had been erected near the entrance to any visitor to site those lifts were to be fitted, it was torture!

Each install team was given two floors to complete, Slim and Alec 'the mad monk' set about the task, and I was their designated skivvy. Which involved carrying radiators, literally miles of various sizes of copper pipe, along with bags of fittings. In between these tasks, I watched these highly skilled engineers install the heating systems.

Although two 'very large spanners' were about to be thrown into the works, the first 'spanner' being a slight engineer's error of floor levels, this involved level 1 & 3 being piped up, 3 should have been 2!

So, when the time came to pressurise the system with cold water, there was an entire floor with a lot of pipes not connected to the other floor, these were known as 'open ended' pipes. Needless to say, there was a LOT of water, this wasn't a bad thing to be honest, as it removed the vast amount of dust that a derelict building gathers over decades.

The second 'spanner' was the developer went into liquidation a few days after we'd installed the heating systems, and were carrying out the final commissioning.

This left all of the companies involved with a hefty materials and labour bill unpaid, to which sadly, a few of the smaller companies involved went bust.

BG being such a huge company managed to swallow the loss, but not without removing all of the materials that had been installed. Therefore, everything had to come out, this meant the radiators, pipes, and boilers had to come down...without the assistance of the lift that had finally been installed, because the electricians had removed their cabling before we went back to remove our stuff.

I tore the poster down of the lift, and threw it in the skip!

CHAPTER ELEVEN
Turv & Wedge

The reason I am writing this episode with two engineers together is because that's how they were, they were one of the three 'two-man' teams we had as installers in Witney depot.

Installers were a different breed to the rest of the engineers, these men were physically as strong as oxen, and without a doubt earnt their crust. The job was physically demanding on every part of the body, especially the knees and the back (as I sit here typing this, my knees are aching after doing an installation a couple of days ago, I feel their pain at 50 years old).

Despite wearing knee pads, and other forms of PPE (Personal Protective Equipment), your body still slowly wears out in this line of work.

Turv was a huge bloke, almost like a blue barn with a ginger beard, he was truly menacing, infact, if Turv were a Viking, his foes would've laid down their weapons immediately, and ran screaming to the hills. He was balding, with ginger whisps of hair reaching out from the sides of his head like copper wires (I imagined lightning dancing through them as he worshipped Thor).

He had small sunken eyes that darted about under two large bushy ginger eyebrows, and although slightly shorter than Stef he had a frame that matched. He wasn't built for speed, but his mind was, he was as sharp as a tac with his quick wit and banter. He had a heart of gold, and this I can say was the same for every engineer in the depot, it was part of the makeup of being a BG Engineer.

Wedge was a lot shorter than Turv, with mousey brown hair and a moustache that sat above a mouth with teeth like tomb stones. His frame may have been smaller, but his strength was incredible. Wedge was built for speed, in body and mind, he and Turv shared the same banter, which sometimes got a bit close to the knuckle.

My first of many memories of these two 'wind up' merchants were when they informed me about my 'initiation ceremony' in my first week, I guess my cheeky schoolboy innocence had to be broken, to reveal a young man, fit enough to stand with these men. I asked them what it entailed, to which Turv replied "Never you mind my boy, you'll know once we grab you!", with Wedge smiling like a wide mouthed frog he added "you get Boss white smeared on your bollocks for a starter!".

Boss White was a pipe jointing paste that we would smear on threaded fittings, and pipe, to ensure it was gas or water tight. It was a sandy coloured, gloopy substance with a faint aroma of fish, that if you accidentally got it on your clothes, it would never wash out. The thought of this around my nut sack filled me with dread, although due to my lateness in maturing, sticking to hair down there would never have been an issue until I was 19.

For the first six months of my apprenticeship, I lived in fear of them getting me. If I was in the depot stores, I always had two routes of escape planned, I would first check on their whereabouts before carrying out my apprentice duties.

They never got me, I found out later, it was just a way to tame the new boy, and that nobody had ever succumbed to such treatment by any gas engineer...ever. A year later, three new apprentices were dealt the same blow as Turv & Wedge passed by.

They then sought my advice asking what would happen, I replied "Never you mind mate, you'll know once they grab you!".

Well, I wasn't going to be the only one falling for it.

CHAPTER TWELVE

The Technicians

These men were the Rolls Royce of engineers within BG, their knowledge of appliances, and central heating systems was astonishing, they were a walking version of an internet search engine (that was nowhere to be seen in 1988), these men could repair and rectify any issues, that would leave the average gas engineer weeping in the back of their van.

Witney depot had three of these geniuses… JP, Spit Spot, and last but definitely not least A Lever. Each one stationed at the end of the locker desks of the engineers, like a full stop at the end of a font of knowledge.

As mentioned, before, they had a 'microfiche' on their desk, this piece of kit would allow them to look at diagrams that included part numbers using microfilm inserts, you needed a degree in physics to understand how the things worked to start with, so this was down to the Technicians to use.

They all donned silvery grey trousers to denote their 'rank', yet they kept the same-coloured shirts as the engineers, all three of them were different in stature, but all immaculately dressed.

CHAPTER THIRTEEN

JP

JP was of average height, with athletic build (due to him being a tennis coach in his spare time), with similar looks to that of the famous film star Gene Wilder. He too had fair hair, by this I meant light, not that he had purchased it from the fair.

His moustache was immaculate, as was his dress code, his work shoes gleaming with polish. There are so many fond memories I have of JP (along with the rest of the depot) that if I chose to write about all of them, I would need to write volumes of these books, rather than this one (okay maybe two). Here are two of my memories...

Memory 1 – BG had a lot of customers, all from different walks of life, the majority were working class general public, and some were Lords, Ladies, Dukes & Duchesses. Witney depot's work area/ patch included Blenheim Palace, situated in Woodstock (approx. 10 miles away), and is home to The Duke of Marlborough, but also the home of the late, great, Sir Winston Churchill.

The majestic stately home was set in walled grounds, with acres of woodland, lush green pastures for sheep and cattle to graze, rivers and lakes, one of which was a boating lake with a bridge carving it in half like a knife through a cake, allowing the duke's staff to keep the boaters in one place, and not go off on a jolly through the extensive and beautifully kept waterways.

JP oozed rapport, he could have been sent into a war-torn country, and within minutes a peace agreement would have been sorted, and a party with all ex-foes dancing and drinking together. The rapport worked in mysterious ways, so much so, that JP was chosen by the duke to oversee any works that were needed to be carried out in the palace, or any of its tied cottages within the grounds. There were also a vast number of properties owned by the duke, outside of the grounds that BG serviced and maintained, but any engineer could carry out that work.

Due to JP's rapport, all BG engineers had access to the grounds, not all at once, and definitely not the palace without JP. Consequently, if you were working in Woodstock and fancied a beautiful view as you ate your sandwiches, you could drive up to the entrance and state that you were reading the gas meter, then sail through without an eyebrow being raised, or charged a penny.

On this one particularly beautiful, and very hot sunny summer day in July, JP was working in Woodstock, and like many other engineers he decided to spend his lunch break in the palace grounds. Having met all of the staff, they waved him through like royalty, ensuring any tourists were moved out of the way to allow this man his right of passage.

JP parked his van on the grass, and decided due to the heat, that being close to water would make him feel cooler, sandwiches, newspaper and flask in hand he made his way to the boating jetty, waved at the man in his hut, and proceeded to climb into one of the boats.

He pushed away from the jetty, and was soon out of harm's way and taking in the sights of families sat on the bank with picnics, with the calming sound of the water lapping against the hull of the tiny boat, as water boatmen skipped in random patterns through the water.

In the meantime, he ate his sandwiches, washing them down with his flask of tea, as he read the paper, he glanced at his watch, he had half an hour left.

After his morning work of servicing gas boilers, and now with a full belly, he made the decision to have a little, and well-earned siesta. His eyelids heavy, he only had three boilers left to service, what an easy afternoon he thought as he drowsed off.

He woke from his slumber to the sound of shouting, blissfully unaware of the time, he glanced up to see the boat keeper aiming his voice towards him with cupped hands, he couldn't hear him clearly as he was too far away, he glanced at his watch, rubbed his eyes in disbelief, it was 4:30pm! He'd been asleep for 3 hours, and still had 3 boilers to service, he grabbed the oars and rowed to the shore, if there had been someone with a stopwatch, he would've been entered into the Olympics rowing team.

He got home at 7pm that evening, with a very good sun tan on his face and arms.

Memory 2 – As an apprentice, the first thing you learn is to show no fear. There is a simple reason for this, there are a large bunch of 'hairy arsed' gas engineers that will make your life, hmm shall I say...very interesting, if they found out you had a fear of something.

Sadly, JP despite his standing within our depot, had an Achilles heel, the engineers found this out due to yours truly informing them about a particular incident.

Unbeknownst to me being a 1st year apprentice I had mentioned to Mickle that we had serviced a boiler, when JP noticed something, and fled the building. I didn't realise that Mickle would then pass on this information, and within a few hours JP's weakness was known. I had no idea of the repercussions of what would happen, although I soon became a very quick learner.

It was a very dark and murky Autumnal morning, leaves blowing about as I walked to work in my BG issued raincoat, despite having a hood, the rain stung my face. The depot came into view, the lights were on, with the windows steamed up, this was such a welcoming sight, I immediately felt warm.

I hung my jacket up in the cloakroom, and proceeded to go about my apprentice duties of making the tea and coffee, before sorting through fittings in the stores.

Some engineers would collect their tea, or coffee, from the kitchen, but the majority were stood at their lockers, sorting through their days job sheets. I took the technicians tea to their desks, JP on this occasion had just arrived, so he received 5-star service of a hot cuppa just as he was seated.

He noticed a match box on his desk, picked it up and shook it, bewildered as to why there was an empty matchbox on his desk, he opened it.

Now to this day, I have no idea who had managed to fit such an enormous spider into such a small space!? The arachnid now free from its dark prison cell, unfolded its legs at speed and flung itself to freedom in the direction of JP, he shrieked at a pitch similar to a woman in a horror film, to which everyone's attention was drawn to him, and in his panic to get away, his tea left the comfort of his mug, and reached the desk of Jim.

Wiping his paperwork, he didn't even flinch, just tapped his pipe, and continued his work.

JP left the depot like a shot, and sat in his van for some considerable time, as the engineers laughed at the morning's entertainment. He ventured back in, after insisting I search the surrounding area and give him the 'all clear', the spider was never found, but to appease his heart rate (and our ear drums), he was ensured it had been let loose on some grass at the back of the yard.

It never happened again, the culprit was never found, and JP had threatened us all with a painful death if it reoccurred.

CHAPTER FOURTEEN
Spit Spot

Spit Spot was a man of very slight build, with dark hair. If he had of grown his hair into a 'bob', he would have been mistaken for a giant match, or after being electrocuted, a chimney sweeps brush.

His spindly frame would have stood no chance in a strong gale if it weren't for the BG issued steel toe cap shoes that we all wore. If he took them off, you could have slid him under a door to let someone in after they lost their keys. Having said that, his great sense of humour, and large friendly persona made up for the size of his body, and in all fairness, I was the same build until I hit 40.

It was an overcast spring morning, it was windy, the cherry blossoms were blown from the trees, and thrown into the air like an invisible crowd hurling confetti at an invisible wedding. Infact, let me change that...Mother Nature was very grumpy, not to the point of a Hurricane force tearing rooves off houses, and uprooting trees (that a BBC weatherman assured us all the previous year we weren't having) but it was definitely a bit of a struggle to ride/push my Honda ER 50cc motorbike to the depot.

Yes people, I had ascended from foot patrol, to mechanised grace after a few months of working for a living. Although, mechanised wasn't actually that much of a bonus for me, as the motorbike in question was 'air cooled' and if I rode it too far it would overheat, and stop running. I think I spent more time pushing the damn thing than riding it, my experience was about to change.

I pushed my 'exercise' motorbike up to the depot wall, kicked the stand down, and walked in to perform the usual tea and coffee ritual. I was met by a gaggle of grumpy engineers in 'my' kitchen, grumbling that there was no milk, and that nobody was sorting it out. I acted on my instinct of fight or flight, which of course was flight (as an apprentice this was natural) and I strolled over to the depot clerk, explained the problem and requested some 'petty cash' to allow me to purchase some milk to calm the masses.

She was an understanding lady, she could see the look of urgency on my face, also reminding me of the sorrowful sight she had witnessed of me, on more than one occasion, pushing my motorbike to work. She dangled a set of keys on a fluffy pink keyring, and started to sway them like a hypnotist, as she said "You want to borrow my moped?".

The hypnotism must have worked, as the next minute I remember pootling along on her moped. This machine was just a simple 'pull the throttle and go', whilst you were sat on a large spongy seat with both feet together on a platform...this was a girls moped, commonly known as a 'sit up and beg' bike.

My bike was a man's 50cc bike, you had to swing your leg over, use a 'kick start', it had big wheels, with 'knobbly' tyres for that perfect 'off road' experience. However, this girl's bike had an electric start, a storage compartment for any urgent milk purchases, no need to push it either, as it was water cooled...and it was 90cc!

I only found this out as I pulled out of the petrol station forecourt, with my valuable liquid cargo onboard, and met with four lads on 50cc road bikes (not the same make as mine, as they would've been stood by their bikes, not sat on them revving the crap out of them! These were smaller versions of moto-racing bikes) at a set of traffic lights. They all glanced across at me, as I pulled in between them, I could see them all looking me up and down, incoherently calling across to each other and laughing at the pink keyring.

Their laughter soon turned to tears, as the lights changed, I pulled the throttle back on my 'cissy mobile' leaving them in the wake of my 90cc kick arse moped! As I indicated into the industrial estate on Station Lane, they were but a distant blur in my mirrors,

I was impressed, but never to the point I would trade my push/ motorbike in for a 'hair dryer on wheels'.

Handing the keys over to the depot clerk, I completed the task of making 25 cups of tea and coffee, to which I had mastered this to a fine art by now. Once this task was done, along with other previously mentioned menial tasks. I was then designated an engineer, or in this case a technician...Spit Spot.

The job for the day we had to replace a damaged flue liner (a flexible chimney pipe) on a Potterton Kingfisher floor standing boiler (this very same appliance nearly killed me in my latter years), I ventured to the store to collect the flue liner, premix mortar, along with the ladders required to complete the job.

The flue liner lay there, like a silver stainless steel tethered serpent, its ends taped to prevent its open mouth from lacerating and losing not necessarily a limb, but definitely a finger or two if unleashed. It was tamed by a black polythene bag, all of which I loaded onto the back of the van.

Not long after battling to close the van doors, Spit Spot appeared out of the store doors, the wind at this point tore them open, making him look like a super hero....'PIPE CLEANER MAN' would have befitted him no problem at all.

The look on his face dashed my image, as he drew a wry smile on his face as he shouted "Nice day to fly a kite Smythe!". We collected the ladders from the ladder store, a small caged area next to the main store, it was almost like an enclosure for endangered ladders it was that secure. We tied them to the top of the van, and sought refuge from the violent gusts in the van, as we set off to our destination...a road called Pensclose, in Witney.

We arrived at the address, a detached bungalow, where we were met by an elderly lady stood in her garden waving a handkerchief at us like a deranged 'Morris dancer'.

Before we exited the van, Spit Spot said "there'll be plenty of tea here Smythe my boy, after you've finished up on the roof", before I had chance to question this newly appointed role as a roofer, he'd gone, hugging the lady like they were long lost relatives that had just been introduced for the first time.

I grabbed the tool roll, and dust sheet from the back of the van, and was caught by a sudden gust of wind, which inflated the dust sheet, transforming it into a billowing sail, I was at its mercy as my 8 stone frame stood no chance. I became a ship without a rudder, and was blown into the front door, then into the hallway. I kept my balance as the audience watched in silent wonder, steadied myself, strode into the kitchen as if nothing had happened, placing the dust sheet down, and unravelling the tool roll.

Once Spit Spot and the lady had finished their chat and supping tea, he explained that the metal liner that was attached to the boiler had corroded in the chimney, therefore the boiler was 'spilling' potentially lethal fumes into the property, so had to be replaced.

This involved using a hammer and bolster on the chimney top to remove the existing securing plate, and GC1 terminal, (a metal designed chimney pot sealed at the top, but with slits in the sides to allow for fumes to exit, but prevent birds from entering the flue system) sealed with a lot of mortar.

We both ventured out into 'Mother Nature's Fart Fest', showing no sign of calming, we assembled the ladders for my route onto the roof, ensuring all was secure. I was handed a bucket with a lump hammer, and then guided onto the ladder. I ascended the ladder at a speed to what probably looked to onlookers like an astronaut taking steps onto the moon's surface, this soon changed as the wind was blowing in my favour, I reached the summit of the roof in no time.

It took very little time in cracking the mortar to reveal the securing plate, I removed the GC1 and fortunately for me I avoided breathing in the mortar dust...as my watery eyes managed to capture most of it, thus rendering me temporarily blind. I sat down on the ridge of the roof, my eyes streaming, adhering to the golden rule not to rub your eyes as the sand/grit would erode your eyes, tears will help clean your eyes, and the sand/grit will wash away...I sat there weeping.

As my nose decided to join in with the flowing of fluid, Spit Spot had scaled the ladder, took the bucket, and guided me down. We both arrived on 'terra firma', me looking like an old wise man with my 'snot tash'. The lady passed me her hanky to clean myself up, a towel would have been more suitable as I mopped my 'fizzog', I handed the tear/snot-soaked hanky back to her, to which she (so rightly so) handled it with thumb and forefinger, despatching it instantly into the garden incinerator close by.

My vision returned, I focused on Spit Spot holding a pair of safety goggles in one hand (hind sight is great, so is health and safety), and the coiled serpent in the other. He placed the liner on the lawn as he handed me the goggles, I proceeded up the roof to the chimney breast donning my eye protection, by this time the wind had subsided a little.

In the meantime, Spit Spot was cutting through the old flue liner attached to the boiler, ready for separation. I heard the faint echo of his voice proclaiming he had severed the liner, so I began to haul the rotten worm from its lair, pulling with all my might, there was an element of resistance, I was determined this wouldn't defeat me, so continued to pull.

The resistance eased suddenly, as I walked backwards along the ridge tiles, I heard a muffled groan as I evacuated the liner from the comfort of the chimney. As the tail of the liner appeared, so did Spit Spot from the back door, coughing and spluttering, brushing the soot from his hair and clothes, he gazed up at me, with bewilderment, looking like a Victorian urchin with his face covered in soot.

I walked back along the ridge of the roof with my coiled metal catch, and made my way down the ladder, as I lowered it down to Spit Spot, he grabbed it from me and started to descend, at that point in time the wind picked up, and he descended in 'fast forward', reaching the lawn like a rocket returning to earth in re-entry, although his arse wasn't on fire, the flue pipe he was clutching onto belched the sudden impact, and covered him in second coat of soot, he removed his jumper, shaking it furiously, placing it on the lawn.

Stifling my laughter, I descended the ladder, to be met by the lady bringing out refreshments, she was a bit unstable on the uneven ground with her slipper boots, the wind again whipped up, causing her apron to fly up and cover her head, before any of us could reach her, and in a moment of panic she emptied the contents of the cups over Spit Spots jumper, before pulling the apron down gasping for air. Once she had regained her composure, she apologised profusely, and scuttled back in declaring a fresh brew was on its way.

Spit Spot looked at me, I looked at him, we looked at his jumper, it was like an example of a washing machine detergent ad prior to the magic being performed to bring it out pristine, but no powder, or liquid on the planet could sort that out, it was ruined. There was no other option, with heads bowed, we had a fake funeral as it joined the hanky in the incinerator.

I grabbed the new liner, put it over my shoulder, safety goggles in place, Spit Spot handed me his pocket knife, and I ventured once more up the ladder to the chimney. I was even more grateful for the safety goggles as Spit Spot entered the bungalow, the air movement spat a plume of soot out of the chimney like a baby volcano, and covered me with the remnants of soot. I placed the tip of the liner in the chimney, allowing about 3 feet into the hole, I removed the knife, and cut through the string, the coil unfurled, the wind howling around me.

I wouldn't be beaten, my bladder decided to contact my brain, stating it had had enough liquid and needed to empty, I ignored it as I started to spin the liner around my head, creating a corkscrew effect, catching my jumper several times on the chimney to steady myself, the liner arrived at the base of the chimney and the top of the boiler, where Spit Spot was guiding it in.

With around 2 foot of the liner protruding at the top, I called down the tube "everything ok?" to which Spit Spot replied "All good Smythe". The clamp was secured on the top, along with the new GC1 terminal, I weatherproofed it with a bucket of mortar, and my trowel, ensuring my initials 'SS' and date, were in place for generations of pigeons to defecate on, or another person to bear witness to the work we had done.

I returned to the lawn, removing my eroded, soot stained, and mortar covered jumper, realising it was irreparable, I cursed under my breath, said my goodbyes, and placed it in the incinerator.

The incinerator ate well that morning.

I ventured inside, Spit Spot was advising the lady that he was about to be carrying out a 'flue flow and spillage' test on the boiler with its brand-new flue, and that all doors must be kept closed whilst this was being carried out as it involved lighting a few smoke matches. If this proved successful, and the smoke ventured up the flue, then a smoke pellet or two would be lit to ensure the fumes from the boiler would follow the same route up the flue, and not into the lungs of the occupants of the bungalow, deeming them......DEAD.

Any interruption in this could mean the test failed, especially due to the adverse weather conditions, and the boiler would need to remain turned off for her safety.

She assured us she would remain in the living room, but was unsure of her husband and the dog's arrival time after he had gone to get the paper, and could be any time as he was a chatterbox. Spit Spot said the test would take about 20 minutes, the woman was uncertain, so I was posted as guard by the back door to ensure the gentleman & pooch wouldn't disrupt this life saving test.

The unfortunate thing here was, as Spit Spot lit the smoke matches, my bladder decided once more to contact my brain, stating if I didn't empty it immediately, then it would have no choice but to empty itself no matter where I was, it had had enough liquid and needed to empty.

As the match smoke flew up the flue, I clocked an open door opposite me stating 'toilet' in a ceramic rectangle with a hand painted toilet on it, my bladder was twitching. I could hold it no more, I glanced up the garden path, there was no sign of the man & dog, I bolted for the loo, closed the door, and I swear to this day I possibly peed for about 10 minutes.

In the meantime, one man and his dog had returned from mowing a meadow, with no guard to prevent their access! The back door swung open fully, and the 3 smoke pellets that had been lit by Spit Spot found an easier exit than the new flue.

As I exited the loo, the 'Fog of War' descended, encapsulating us all as it slowly crept out through the back door no lower than waist height, we were all coughing and spluttering, as I lowered to gain fresh air, I could see the dog rolling about near the boiler, hoping it wasn't having a seizure, and thinking this was like a scene from a horror film, the thought vanished rapidly, so did the smoke as the woman opened the living room door.

Thankfully the smoke from the pellets didn't cause too much harm, this however was a different matter for the dog ironically called 'sooty', as he had decided he liked the smell of soot on Spit

Spots dust sheet, and was rolling in it...until the smoke cleared, and he had been rumbled!

He knew he was in trouble, and set off like an out-of-control firework...'nutmegging' the lady (a football term for when a footballer kicks the ball between the goalie's legs to score) and becoming a furry pinball, bouncing around their cream sofas and chairs.

This is the first time I believe I had encountered Tourette's, as the lady released a volley of words that I couldn't repeat at such a young age.

However, I'm older now and it went like this...

"George, if you don't catch that f*cking dog, it's having your f*cking dinner, and you're going in the f*cking incinerator along with my hanky & their jumpers' you t*sspot!"

After masses of apologies by the customers for disrupting our tests, we re-tested the boiler & flue, it passed, we tidied up our sheets, loaded the van up, and said our goodbyes.

Sooty was caught, George wasn't incinerated, the boiler was safe... job done.

I just had a thought as I write this...my initials are S.S.

I hope that one day historians don't think that Nazi tyranny was prevalent as an underground movement in Witney at that time! Ok, maybe I'm over thinking this, or, maybe I need another beer?

Love you Mr. Potter...God Save the Queen!

CHAPTER FIFTEEN

A Lever

A Lever (AL) was the largest build of the Technicians, their knowledge was equal, but A Lever was taller with chiselled looks, jet black hair and olive skin. His dress code was the same as JP and Spit Spot...immaculate.

My first experience of working with AL was when I'd been with BG a few weeks, I'd built a small amount of experience up, to the point where I knew the specific tools, fittings, and materials that were required by an engineer, this particular time, there's a couple of tools that have left me scarred...physically and mentally.

We were given the wonderful task of preparing a new housing estate called Rowell Way, in Chipping Norton, for the installation of central heating systems, otherwise known as '1st fix' (this involved fixing the boiler to the wall, and installing pipework from the gas and water supplies to the boiler).

We arrived on site in the BG Maestro Van, windows down as 'air con' was a myth in those days. The weather was almost tropical, sun shining with bright blue skies, and a large amount of humidity in the air, to the point where you would sweat just by blinking.

As we exited the blue & white 'oven' and were met by the site foreman, his name escapes me, but his nickname didn't. He was 'bon-bon', named because he was round, had very bad dandruff, and had a sickly-sweet smell about him, very much like the sweet we all knew as kids. He directed us across to the current properties that needed the work, we gathered materials from the lockup and made our way over to the first house.

AL produced from his tool box, a template of the boiler fixing bracket, a lump hammer, and a strange looking metal peg called a 'rawl plug jumper'. He explained that he would do the first one, maybe two, then I could take over doing the rest of them, as you can imagine I was absolutely over the moon to be given the responsibility, this would soon change.

The template was in place on the designated wall, the drill holes marked, and lump hammer grasped firmly in AL's hand. Looking around, I wondered how we were going to make the holes to put the 'plugs and screws' in, considering there was no electrical sockets anywhere to be seen (this was an era that hadn't yet discovered the 'cordless' drill age).

Behold the 'rawl plug jumper' RPJ...not to be confused with the military RPG, as that knocks a larger hole in a lot of things!

This was lifted aloft, and placed on the marked stonework, and in one fell swoop of the lump hammer AL drove the peg half way in, twisted it, and knocked it fully home, with a final twist he pulled the RPJ out. Lining it up with the next mark, he repeated this for the three remaining required holes. I thought to myself how easy this is going to be, I would barely break a sweat.

We moved onto the next property, AL carrying the tools, as I followed at his heels with the paper template. Once completed, he turned to me and asked "Ok with this Spikey boy?", he had barely broken a sweat, so I was adamant that I was the new man/boy for the job.

A Lever dropped the tools off at the next property, and even got his step ladder out of the van for me as I was (and still am) vertically challenged. I picked up the RPJ in my left hand, and the lump hammer in my right hand, taken aback by the weight of the hammer, how could it be SO heavy having just seen A Lever swinging it about like a tooth pick? I gathered my 16-year-old thoughts and strength, and swung the hammer toward its target, it was a 'bullseye'! It bounced off, a small cloud of dust emanating from my first strike, as the dust cleared, I had barely marked the stone.

As I lifted the hammer for a second strike and swung, AL poked his head round the corner to ask how things were, the hammer changed trajectory, and proceeded to mulch part of my hand. Both implements hit the floor, as I felt my heart beating in my left hand.

The pain travelled around for a while; however, I was young, and years of fighting, falling off bikes, swings, go karts, playing British Bulldog, bundles, piggy back fights, rugby, Freddy fowlers football & stone fights had hardened me to pain.

He had almost predicted/realised my plight, as my steel toe capped shoes were probably the heaviest part of me, therefore, a new 'knocking stick' appeared, a very much lighter claw hammer. Despite its lightweight appearance, its destructive capability was similar, the only down side to this hammer was it had a smaller surface area of head to strike the RPJ. This I found out after three strikes…1 HIT….2 HIT…3 SHIT!

The head hit my forefinger knuckle with a direct hit, the pain was of a smaller area than the lump hammer, but far more intense, similar to a shin strike at football/hockey (yes, I played hockey at school) with low socks and no shin pads, it's a pain nothing like a punch on the nose…it was worse.

With my defunct throbbing hand, I was as much use to AL as a handbrake on a canoe, and the rest of the afternoon was spent with me passing AL tools.

We had safety gloves, but they were far too cumbersome to allow us to carry out any work of this variety, and to this day I have an indent in my left forefinger knuckle to prove it.

I worked with AL on a few occasions, one of which we needed to measure the size of a room, so he swung me by my ankles around a room to gauge the size, he of course knew the room was far bigger than me attached to his outstretched arms, he just wanted to scare me.

The final time we worked together, was when I was a 3rd year apprentice, my final year before I was released into the wild/district. As part of my final assessments (along with exams at college) a technician was assigned to carry out stringent tests to ensure I was competent to carry out my duties as a qualified gas engineer for BG.

I have to say AL was a different man on those days, very strict, with no joking or banter, this I understood, and so rightly so.

Thanks to the guidance of Martin, the depot clerks, ALL of the engineers, JP & Spit Spot, my college lecturers: Mr. Terry Summers, Mr. Bob Edmunds (R.I.P.), Mr. Lyn Jones, and last but not least AL.

You made my life fun, hard, and sometimes harsh...but mainly fun.

Now let the adventures commence...

Be free my beauty!

CHAPTER SIXTEEN
O.A.P. 'Electrocution' lesson

It was a glorious summers day, not a cloud to be seen, just a beautiful blue sky with the sun beaming down. This meant shades on, windows down in my BG emblazoned Maestro van, radio playing, as I drove through the town centre of Woodstock, admiring the view of the numerous tourists 'snapping' pictures with their cameras (no mobile phones in those days).

Life was good…

I arrived at my final job for the day, an annual service of a gas boiler in a house situated in a small cul de sac, far from the madding crowds of 'happy snappers'. Grabbing my tool roll, folder, dust sheet, and Henry vac (it's a vacuum cleaner, not a Hoover…as that's a brand name, not the description…Murley! Love you mate) I rang the doorbell and an elderly lady appeared from behind her net curtain, and beckoned me in.

As I walked into the living room, and began to introduce myself, the lady completely ignored me, and squealed "why are you this early? I booked you for after 3pm!", I was completely taken aback by this, and nervously glanced at my watch, it was 3:45pm.

Before I had chance to explain the time zone that we were both in, she beckoned me once more, almost like she was wanting me to follow her to reveal hidden treasure. I followed her into the kitchen to be confronted by everything covered in bed sheets, apart from the windows, and a floor standing Potterton Kingfisher gas boiler, everything was covered!

It was quite eerie, pretty similar to a film where the haunted mansion has all the furniture covered to protect it. The only difference being this was a two bedroom 'Dorma' bungalow (this is a bungalow that has had the loft converted into bedrooms, and windows added into the roof) so the question being, why so many bed sheets? This never concerned me after the events that were about to unfold.

She sensed my surprise of seeing so much linen, and spoke for the first time "I've put these sheets down, as last year it was a bit sooty, boiler's off, I won't offer you a cup of tea as you're early". Her voice was so high pitched that I feel if you wanted to carry out a survey of bats in the vicinity, or, set the dogs off barking for a 20-mile radius just stand her in a field and ask her to talk.

She may have also been responsible for my hearing condition of Tinnitus that I've developed over the last 10 years, and absolutely nothing at all to do with years of using hammer drills. Or, dancing at raves, and night clubs, walking home with my ears still ringing.

I replied "ah, it won't be too bad this year, I'm sure. No problem with the tea, are you sure it's off?"

"Yes, it's off" she replied.

I laid my dust sheet on top of the layers of existing dust sheets, plugged Henry in, and set about cleaning out the boiler. Relying on the information the lady had given me; I checked the wires were 'dead', then removed the power cable consisting of 3 wires...

Brown – Live (Electricity coming from the power station).

Blue – Neutral (Used electricity going back to the power station).

Green & Yellow – Earth (A protective cable that saves lives, and sends the devil's tickling stick back to the ground).

I began to carry out the cleaning of the boiler, suddenly feeling some discomfort in my abdominal region, I chose to ignore it. Pleased with my job of cleaning, with no sign of soot, I began to re-assemble the boiler, all was going well until I grabbed the power cable for the boiler.

What I was about to experience can best be described as a very large hamster nibbling at your fingers…as the surge of electricity pulsed through my body, from my right hand holding the cable, to my left hand holding the casing of the boiler, my chest muscles pulsing like I was trying to impress the crowds at a 'Mr. Universe' contest…

Roll back 14 hours…I'd been out with my mates, drinking pints of John Smith's Bitter and dancing in The Red Lion having the time of my life. It must have been that last 'one' dodgy pint of the six that I'd consumed, as I'd spent a fair bit of time sat on the loo, eventually my arse had stopped spitting 'fizzy gravy' and I'd gone to sleep.

Jump forward to my grip on the power cord, the 240 volts of electricity that were passing through my body had not only decided to perform tricks with my 'pecs', but had also decided to open the 'bomb bay doors'…

Before I could release the cable, it felt like I'd sat in a warm shepherd's pie.

I stood up, hair smoking, boxers full, and walked like 'John Wayne' that had been riding a horse for days, into the lounge.

The lady was sat in her high back chair, watching the TV programme 'Countdown' on Channel 4, the volume so loud that the ornaments were performing dance moves on the mantlepiece.

I piped up "Excuse me, I thought you said it was off?", she fumbled with her remote control, as the 'shepherd's pie' in my boxers was cooling down, and asked me to repeat my question.

"I thought you said it was off?" I repeated, she glanced at the clock as did I, it was 4:10pm.

She said "Oh it comes on at 4", not realising that at some point at 4:05pm I had part of her electricity supply passing through my body…having seen, Jesus, Mary, Joseph, the Donkey, and maybe a few pixies too.

"Do you mind if I use your toilet, please?" I asked, she directed me to a door in the hallway, I walked like I had an invisible pumpkin between my legs into the loo, locked the door, cleaned myself up, and attempted to dispose of the toilet roll, along with my boxer shorts into the pan of sin.

I pulled the flush handle, praying that the volume of water flowing would take away the evidence, due to my atheist beliefs I was on a hiding to nothing, this proved true after the second flush attempt, and the water touching the brim of the pan, the 'package' was going nowhere.

I decided that my best plan of attack was to...

Leave the property as quickly as possible, and say nothing...sorry, but she'd almost killed me, and never made me a cuppa!

A complaint came in a few days later, but after explaining my issues of a poorly tummy due to a bug that I'd picked up (ok, I bent the truth a little) the investigation was dropped, as prior to this I had a gleaming record with customer satisfaction cards coming in with 5* reviews.

The best tip I can give you is NEVER trust a customer, and always check the electricity is off yourself...or wear a nappy!

CHAPTER SEVENTEEN
Chim, Chim-a-ney...Chim, Chim-boom!

It was a fine sunny summer morning in the shire with white fluffy clouds barely moving in a beautiful blue sky, days like this I felt so happy to be alive, and still do, you don't need money to appreciate this.

The village of Tackley was my destination, a beautiful and serene village tucked away just past Woodstock, venturing past Sturdy's Castle, the infamous 'spud' pub and turned down the lane that would lead to the village.

As a young engineer my right foot was quite often equipped with an imaginary 'diver's boot', therefore speed was of the essence, and not my safety.

I hurtled down the single track into the village at a speed similar to a rocket re-entering the earth's atmosphere, only to be met by a very large tractor with a very large farmer in the cab heading toward me, a lot slower, but a lot more solid than my G reg Austin Maestro van!

I hit the brakes and anchored up, dust and smoke billowing from the road and my tyres...closing my eyes waiting for the impact... only to open them after a few seconds to see no tractor!? I looked around completely perplexed, and spotted he'd turned into a field, smirking and giving me the 'V' sign that was nothing at all like a token of peace, but the taunt of an English archer. Slightly shaken, I decided to slow my driving down, and took on the guise of a milk float as I continued with my journey.

I reached the cul de sac, gathered my tool roll, dust sheet

and trusty 'Henry' vacuum (Murley), still reeling from my own stupidity of driving recklessly for a second, this was soon to change.

As I pressed the doorbell the 'plinkety-plink' of a very sad version of 'Greensleeves' came from somewhere inside the house, and shortly after, a tall man appeared, by that I mean he was TALL he must have been close to 7 feet! as he bowed down under the front door threshold to greet me, I craned my neck to look up (granted my 5ft 7in frame was almost of the 'Hobbit' class therefore deemed mildly vertically challenged) taken aback by his size, I spluttered " Good morning Sir, British Gas, I'm here to service your warm air heater".

He would be known as Goliath, he glanced around behind me, and queried "Are you on your own?", I could feel myself glowing with embarrassment, knowing full well that at 19 years old, despite being a fully qualified gas engineer, I had no wrinkles, a full head of 'super gel' spikey hair, two gold earrings, and donning a pristine uniform, and tool kit.

This of course is completely different in every aspect of the older type of engineer, who had wrinkles, no gel in their hair, and had a lot more muscle mass than my 9½ stone framework.

"Yes sir, I'm the engineer, there is no one else" my confidence back on track, I asked where the heater was, and followed him into the hallway, opening a door with vents fitted he revealed the heater. It was a Bamforth, this was nothing like the majority of heaters I had serviced, but very similar in design.

"Seen one of these old devils before have you son?" the customer enquired, "No problem at all sir, leave it with me, I can do these blindfolded" I instantly replied, my confidence was overwhelming.

"I'll leave you to it, I'll be in the garden if you need me, ok?" said the now assured man/Goliath, "absolutely fine sir, I'll come and find you when I'm done", he left me to it.

STEVE SMITH

Pause the story...

All Warm Air Heaters are constructed of a big metal box with a smaller box inside called the combustion chamber (CC), a gas burner would sit inside this and heat the CC, transferring heat to the outer box where a fan would blow it around the house via a route of ducts. The fumes from the gas burner would exit via a separate chimney system or 'Flue' to outside, and fresh air needed to allow correct combustion would be taken directly from the room with a vent to outside (that is permanently open).

I won't go into the details of different manufacturers/models of gas appliances as this is a cure for insomnia, and I want to keep my readers glued to the book, not drooling into it, then waking with a crick similar to me looking at this customer. ***Please continue***...

I was adamant I could service this unit, the gas connections to it were the same. I stripped it down, and cleaned every part of it, reassembling it didn't seem a problem.

That was until it came to lighting it.

I lit the pilot light (A small flame that had to heat a safety device before it lit the main burner), however, this unit unlike most heaters, had **two** burners in **two** separate CC's. A primary burner & pilot light, and a secondary burner, the secondary burner had a 'connector pipe' that had to line up with the primary burner.

Here was my first mistake... I turned the controls to ON, and lit the pilot, this then lit the primary burner, and I watched in fascination as the flames erupted into life, dancing inside the chamber, almost hypnotising.

A few seconds passed, then I looked across at the secondary burner which was in darkness "hmm how odd" I thought as I realised the error of my ways, I'd not lined up the 'connector pipe', and before my brain could say:

"DO NOT TAP THE CONNECTOR PIPE INTO PLACE AS THE CHAMBER IS FULL OF UNLIT GAS!" ...

68

Here was my second mistake... I tapped the connector pipe with my spanner...it fell into place.

My Brain said "OOOOOOOOOOOOOOooooooooh SHIT you better duck!", I did, as the second chamber ignited its unburnt gas, it was like I had awakened a sleeping dragon that had severe flatulence too. The eruption of flame travelled up into the flue system, as every door in the house shook, I heard a faint 'pop' as it must have exited out of the top of the flue/chimney pot.

I gained my composure, and glanced at the now perfect flame picture of the two burners, then ventured off to see if the customer was still out of earshot of me cursing my own mishap, and sheer disbelief/praise that I still had hair and eyebrows!

I walked into the kitchen, my heart rate similar to that of a mouse being chased by a cat, and looked through the window, to see Goliath propped up against his garden fork, smoking a fag and looking up at his roof, I tried grabbing his attention by waving, but his gaze was fixed.

I ventured out into his back garden which was a sight to behold, a plethora of flowers, fruits and vegetables, although I was more concerned by the puzzled look on his face, so enquired "lovely garden, everything ok sir?".

He broke his gaze, flicked the ash off his fag, and stated "you can come here again my boy, you've clearly done a good job, as I've never seen soot or flames come out of the top of that pot before, everything ok?"

"Thank you, everything was absolutely fine" my confident mouth said, as my brain was whispering "you f*ckwit" repeatedly.

I finished the other tests, got a signature, and left.

CHAPTER EIGHTEEN
Breaker, breaker, this is baby bear

At the fine age of 21, and with five years' experience under my belt (including my apprenticeship) as an industry trained engineer, I was now eligible to join the ranks of the 'emergency' engineer. I felt so happy being offered this additional string to my bow, also making me feel an honourable member of the family, this was clear that MB had confidence in my abilities.

Their role consisted of dealing mainly with tracing and repairing gas leaks, or carbon monoxide reports (sadly sometimes dealing with a fatality), and being incorporated into the 'out of hours' callout rota.

After very extreme stringent training on the GASCO seeker (an instrument finely tuned to detect gas leaks, like an electronic sniffer dog), and a few weeks of a technician 'shadowing' me, I passed with flying colours.

The criteria of a gas leak are ^:

i) __DO__ turn off your gas supply (a lever next to your meter, pull it down).

ii) __DO__ remove ALL naked flames.

iii) __DO__ open all windows and doors.

iv) CALL EMERGENCY SERVICES ON: 0800 111 999 – if there is a fire call 999 too.

v) __DO NOT__ operate any electrical switches, smoke, vape, or use naked flames.

vi) __DO NOT__ enter/re-enter the property until told to do so.

The callout role consisted of you being available to attend an emergency at any time of the night for a week, here was the rota:

Friday 5pm – Monday 8am.

Mon 5pm – Tues 8am.

Tues 5pm – Wed 8am.

Wed 5pm – Thurs 8am.

Thurs 5pm – Fri 8am…hand the keys to the next engineer.

You would be doing a day's work in your normal working hours, then be ready to go out if you were called on your house phone. If you were called out after midnight, you would have 'sleeping in time' so would therefore return to work at the relevant time to how many hours you had worked after 12.

As this was the 1990's, mobile phones hadn't been invented, therefore part of our equipment (that my now faithful Transit F37 OTR had been kitted out with) was similar to a CB radio (a short band radio set to certain frequencies, that was used by the emergency services, oh, and anyone that could afford it in a council house in the 70's and 80's), which meant we could communicate with our 'emergency' HQ in Oxford, but I'll call it a 'GB' as it was on a completely different frequency (in more ways than one).

The week you were on callout, you were usually on 'emergency' in the day too, to allow you to sleep, but to also follow on from a job that may have been involved with the previous evening.

This particular morning, I received a call over the 'GB' at 08:15, an 'uncontrolled' gas escape at a property in a village called Kidlington.

There are two types of gas escapes:

i)   Uncontrolled – This is where the customer has turned the gas cock off, which is a lever next to their gas meter (now reworded to remove cock, and known as an Emergency Control Valve or ECV) and can still smell gas, we had 1 hour to get to the property.

ii)   Controlled – This is where the customer has turned the gas off at the meter, and can no longer smell gas, we had 4 hours to get to the property.

N.B. both of these would be categorised after following the criteria advised by the telephone operator (as stated above^)

I knew the urgency, and threat to a person/peoples' lives, so gave it the 'divers boot' accelerator to get to the property as soon as possible (I'd never overtake in a town or village, but the country roads and highways I did, no shame felt, peoples' lives were at stake).

I reached the property, gathering my equipment, then knocking on the door with some urgency (not ringing the doorbell as a spark could ignite the suspected gas leak!), within moments a very voluptuous woman answered the door, wearing a dressing gown, she beckoned me in, and locked the door behind me, slipping the key down the front of her dressing gown. I thought nothing of it as I entered the hallway, quite often customers would be in their dressing gowns, and would lock the door for security reasons.

"Good morning Madam, you reported a gas leak, where do you suspect it is?" I said with curiosity, she replied "It's the gas fire in the front room, it stinks" as she shuffled off in her fluffy slippers, I followed, arriving in her front room with the accused gas fire in view. Activating my GASCO seeker, I checked all the necessary pipes and connections, as the lady sat on the sofa watching me with interest.

With no reading of a leak whatsoever, and knowing that this piece of kit was so sensitive it could detect a 'gnat fart' in a stadium. Somewhat perplexed, I stated "nothing here, can I see your gas meter?" to which she replied "oh, I'm not sure actually, it might be the heater up on the landing, but I'll show you the meter".

I followed her lead, and we came to a small cupboard under the stairs, she opened the door and ventured in, turning and beckoned me in with a curl of her finger, I bent down and squeezed into the remaining space, realising it was a bit more 'tighter' than I first assumed, and we both became very snug as we both looked at the gas meter.

I carried out a test at the meter with a piece of kit called a manometer or 'U' gauge, this would ascertain if there was a leak on any of the pipework in the property, it was at this point I could smell Whiskey on her breath, as her gowned breasts rested on my shoulder.

The test takes 3 minutes using the 'U' gauge, it was I have to say the **LONGEST 3** minutes of my life (at that time), and the conversation moved from there was no leak from my point, to did I have a girlfriend from hers.

I exited the cupboard with an element of nervousness about me, I stated that there were no leaks detected, therefore my job was complete.

Her reply was "You're a bit of a 'skinny runt' aren't you? You need feeding up" as she looked me up and down, then whispered "then we'll go upstairs to find the leak on the landing".

Somewhat taken aback, I gazed up the stairs, there was no heater on the landing, so I stated "there is no heater on the landing, I think I'm done here".

"No, no, there's definitely a leak upstairs, go in the front room I'll make you a cup of tea, and some food, then we'll go upstairs" then she vanished into the kitchen, a clutter of crockery sounding off.

I tiptoed to the front door like an assassin evading capture, I tried the door handle, locked. I scuttled back into the front room, trying the windows, locked. I sat on the sofa planning my escape, even thinking of thwacking her with a sofa cushion, although that could only lead to her getting annoyed, and dragging me upstairs after being stunned by a retaliatory strike with another cushion.

She entered with a tray, rattling the contents about as she walked, then sat down beside me. I looked at the contents on the plate, it was possibly a ham ploughmans? It would never have made it to any chef star ratings of ANY pub/restaurant due to the fact that it looked like she'd cut the ham with an axe/chainsaw... "Get that down you, I'll go and make your cuppa, and then we'll go upstairs" she said, trying to be seductive, but her slurred voice was letting her down.

Sat with this banquet/massacre in front of me I glanced at my watch, it was ONLY 09:00, I wasn't hungry, even if it was the afternoon, I felt I still wouldn't be hungry to eat the chunks of carnage in my possession.

I needed an exit strategy... I could hear the kettle's whistle stating it was boiling, I didn't have long before we would be venturing up the 'wooden hill into sheet lane'.

I stood up and deposited the majority of my plate behind the sofa, and sat back down again, just in time as she opened the door bringing in my cuppa. I was sat there with a 'full look' on my face, and partially empty plate. She placed the cup on a table next to me, and took the tray, and placed it on the floor, sitting next to me, the aroma of whiskey was fresh once more as she slurred "we shooould go upshtairs to shee the leak", at this point my plan was hatched, I stated/lied "I need to contact my HQ as it's protocol to contact them every half hour as a matter of safety, or they call the police".

Her eyes slightly glazed, I could almost hear her inebriated cogs in her brain grinding "Ok, I'll let you out, but your tools shtay here!" she removed the key from her cleavage, stood up, and like 'a human pinball' bounced off the walls, giggling as she did, until she reached the front door. After a few very long seconds, the key found the hole, she raised an arm in triumph and squealed as she opened the door, and I saw freedom!

Although I was without my equipment, the smell of the cherry blossoms of the nearby tree made me feel like fleeing. However, I refrained from that, and grabbed the handset of the GB...

Me: "63456 to control, are you receiving, over?"

HQ: "Go ahead 63456, receiving, over"

Me: "No leak found at property, although drunken lady wants me to go upstairs, and she won't let me out until we sort the leak out, my tools are still in the house, over"

At this point I need to explain that our radio system had a good range on it, meaning that **EVERY** engineer could also hear my plight that was in range of the transmission yet they were untraceable. Therefore, the airways were suddenly filled with comments...

"Go on Spikey, boy get in there my son!"

"Let her make a man out of you!"

"Go on boy, give her one from me!"

HQ: (laughter in the background) "Received 63456, we'll call her and make out you have another job, so you need to leave as there's another emergency, over"

I glanced at the customer; she was giving me the drunken one-eyed sniper look of suspicion. As the 'supporting' comments from my colleagues continued through the speaker, I heard her house phone ring. She proceeded to answer, nodding a few times, then hung up.

I walked toward the property, as I reached her front door, she passed me my equipment and stated we would meet again.

"Rest assured madam we won't!" I mumbled under my breath, as I placed my equipment in the front of the van, usually it went in the back of the van, in its designated place…. not today, they went in the front of my cab, as I drove off the drive at speed! I never saw her again.

CHAPTER NINETEEN
I'm not leaving on a jet plane

As an 'emergency' engineer sometimes we had fake emergency gas escapes to attend to, whether it was a bloke reporting a smell from his larder, where it turns out the smell was a mouldy onion. To other examples, a blocked toilet, a teenage boy's rogue 'best friend' sock in a bedroom, to a drunken lady wanting her wicked way with a young engineer. All of which weren't life threatening, apart from the latter one...possibly.

However, the majority of the leaks reported were genuine, I'm unable to give you the exact amount per day that were reported for the following reasons:

i)   I'm an engineer, so didn't monitor the number of calls.

ii)   Even if I did know the amount...I'd never let you know, as it would cause mass panic, and people would stop using gas, and I would be unemployed! Wrong of me to joke at this point?

iii)   There wasn't that many leaks, and nobody died on my watch.

The category of gas leak went out the window whenever somebody reported a smell of gas outside, as this could be a leak from a gas main pipe buried under the road/ grass verge/field, and this was a bit more of a concern to a gasman than Mrs. Jones's occasional smell from her cooker.

Here's a slight insight/non-insomnia description into how you get gas to your properties. The country is covered with a network of underground gas pipes of varied sizes, and pressures (assisted by turbines to ensure the pressure is passed along the network, and it is at the correct temperature to stop it 'chilling'), all very cleverly worked out by very clever people to deliver the correct amount of gas where it's needed.

If there was a leak reported, then this was classed as an 'outsider' and required an immediate response, no matter what time of day, we had to attend.

At this point, I would just like to thank the occasional tosspot who reported a smell of gas from a payphone (before mobiles remember) whilst they were 'pissed as farts' on their way home from a nightclub.

As I would be dragged from my slumber, to drive 20 miles, get the GASCO out, to find nothing, report back, then trundle off home... hoping that the inebriated halfwit who'd reported it was lying in a pool of their own piss.

However, I wasn't ruthless, as I never wished they were outside, but in their own bed, or the girlfriends' bed, at his 'in laws' house.

There are a few incidents that shook me up, some are mentioned in this book, and there are more to follow in my next book. Despite your training, and experience, you learn something new EVERY single day of your life, anyone who denies this is a muppet! This particular episode went like this...

The age of technology was accelerating at a rapid rate, we now had digital mobile handsets in our vans on a private network, the callsigns were still the same.

HQ: "63456 this is HQ, are you receiving over?".

Me: "Roger HQ, receiving, over".

HQ: "Outsider reported at Kidlington airport, fire brigade is in attendance, any idea of E.T.A. (Estimated Time of Arrival)?

Me: "Received, ETA 20 mins, over and out".

It was a crisp and still Autumn morning, with multi-coloured leaves of red, orange, yellow and brown, slowly falling from the trees in almost a submission and countdown to Winter, as I sped toward the airport.

Arriving at the Bladon roundabout, I ventured onto the 3rd exit toward Kidlington to be met by a police car blocking the dual carriageway, I stopped at the 'POLCE STOP' sign, briefly thinking there must've been an accident, and was about to gather my thoughts of a redirection, when a copper appeared out of nowhere beckoning me to him.

I drove past his signage, and wound the window down, I didn't even get chance to say good morning, he blurted out "Drive on until you meet the fire engines, and good luck!" I was completely unaware of what I was about to come up against, but this was a little taster.

I arrived at two fire engines blocking the slip road in a staggered formation, I was met by a fireman who immediately shouted "go see the guv in the white hat", I nodded, grabbing, and wrestling my 'high vis' jacket as I ventured toward the leader of the pack.

The 'Guv' was a stocky fellow, not fat, just built to be able to drag people out of buildings, he had piercing blue eyes and a grey moustache that's all I remember until he opened his mouth and said the following:

"Thank God you're here at last, it's a big leak, we've grounded all aircraft, evacuated a terraced block of houses, and instructed the nearby industrial estates to turn off all machinery, stay inside, and not to smoke, what are your instructions?"

All the time he was explaining this to me there was an ear-piercing roar of a jet plane that was ready to take off on the runway nearby, clearly the pilots were idiots, and surely the safety of their passengers was paramount!?

I enquired "Have you said that plane needs to kill its engines?"

Guv: "What plane?"

Me: "That plane with the engines running"

Guv: "That's not a plane, that's your gas leak!"

Time froze for a few seconds as I stared at the fireman in disbelief...

"I'm sorry could you repeat that?" I said.

"Yes, that's your gas leak, you might need some back up!" he said.

My knees knocked together, I had a nauseous feeling in the pit of my stomach knowing that I was solely responsible for what happened next, it could go two ways 1) lead to this being resolved quickly with no fuss, or (2) making headline news as millions of pounds of aircraft, buildings and fire brigade....and a gasman, explode from a cloud of ignited natural gas.

I contacted HQ requiring immediate assistance from the Distribution gang, as previously stated, these were men of a different ilk, these were fearless men, almost warrior class, who could dig through anything. I truly believe they were badgers in a previous life...warrior badgers.

I also asked for another escape engineer to assist with crowd control on the industrial estate up the road, as I knew that come 11:30am Big Bertha's Burger Van would appear, and the masses would pour out of their industrial units like ants foraging from their nest, and there could be trouble. Herbie was dispatched.

Here's the reason why there could be trouble...

Bertha was a 'well built' lady who smoked more fags than anyone I ever knew, lighting one after the other off the gas grill as she cooked the food, infact I heard through the grapevine that she had bought the van with cigarette loyalty cards from Benson & Hedges, this might be myth, or fact, I never asked.

She made her living by selling cooked food (a term some would contest) to the general public via a small catering van, due to her size, some would whisper that the food was always fresh as she would ensure any leftovers were 'snaffled'.

The van she sold her wares from was, shall we say, a tad too small for her and the cooking equipment inside. Another whisper was, she would use goose fat on the doorway to squeeze in, creating a 'popping' sound as she went in, and out.

Back to the story...

HQ had already taken on board the severity of the leak from the Fire Brigade's call, backed up by my terrified call/sobbing uncontrollably into the mouthpiece of the handset in my van, which I'd like to believe reassured them we needed help asap!

Five minutes later the guys turned up, and after chatting to the fire chief, and looking at the damage, they started to get suited up with fire proof gear and oxygen masks, I decided to leave them to it and join my colleague.

I jumped in the van and drove off to the industrial estate, glancing at my watch, oh crap, it was 11:27am! I put my foot down, and arrived just in time to see my colleague 'Herbie' out of the van with his hi-vis vest on, advising some disgruntled car mechanics to go back to their unit as there were high volumes of gas in the air, and we needed to reduce the risk of ignition.

That all fell by the way-side as Bertha arrived in her van, with a fag in her chops (not her produce, but her mouth), we couldn't hold back the 'hangry' crowd (hungry and angry) as she clanged the bell, it was like a mass exodus as people of all ages raced towards us. We had concern for their lives due to the pockets of gas that were drifting over, but despite numerous warnings, we decided our lives weren't worth risking over a £1 bacon butty.

Herbie's van was closer so we walked over to his to get an update from HQ, Herbie was a more senior engineer, he'd been an emergency engineer long before I had even been thought about by my parents, he knew his stuff.

Herbie: "12864 to HQ, are you receiving over?" ...

Herbie was from the same Shire as me, had the same accent, a 'country bumpkin/farmer' (to which I'm very proud of), this changed when he talked on the handset, he transformed into a radio operator from World War 2, his voice was so posh, it made the Queen sound like a farmer.

HQ: "12864, please repeat as I didn't understand, over"

Herbie sighed, looked at me shaking his head and said "they always do this, do you have the same hassle?"

"Yes, it's to do with the frequency" I lied.

Herbie repeated the question, only a lot slower, and we were instructed to return to the distribution gang.

We arrived back on site, by this time, the fire brigade had left site, and the distribution lads/ badger warriors, were just packing up, one of them walked over carrying a yellow fireman's helmet, this was Mr. Fleet, he was a legend amongst the clan, he tossed the object over and Herbie caught it.

"That's from one of the lads in the brigade, I know you've always wanted one" said Mr. Fleet "Good job it was a cap Herb, we just put another one on, job done".

Herbie was a huge fan of the fire brigade, and he grinned like a 'Cheshire cat' replying "Thanks for this" as he waved his prize "No need to purge & relight then, sounds good to me, see you again Fleety".

Purge & relight - If any gas has escaped from a pipe, and has been repaired, there'll be air in the pipe that needs to be cleared, and without boring you to death with the procedures, the air needs to be cleared through a piece of kit called a flame trap, or more often than not, a gas ring on a cooker or hob.

This is to prevent people lighting a cooker, walking away, then air coming through, extinguishing the flame, to then allow gas to enter once more, but unlit. Thus, causing a potential problem of instantly cooking the chicken, and the occupants of the house.

The whole incident had occurred by a team of men digging trenches for 'NTL fibre broadband' (now Virgin Media), and they'd used a JCB digger to make the trench, but had caught the end 'cap' of a 12" medium pressure gas main that was laid there in preparation for a housing estate, to be built on the airport grounds if it fell into disuse.

The Distribution team resolved this by using a pair of pneumatic powered rollers, that once in place would squeeze down on the plastic pipe to stop the escape (known as a 'squeeze off'), then they would use a plastic welding machine to fit another plastic cap.

Now, usually there are plans of gas, electricity, water and phone line networks that everyone who carried out excavation work had this information, sometimes it wasn't very accurate, and it was down to the 'Badger Warriors' to know where pipes were.

Sadly, NTL were the 'apprentices' of this, and not only did they create this issue, they kept Herbie, me, and Southern Gas very busy throughout their 'essential upgrade'.

In their defence, the plastic pipeline was undetectable by a metal detector called a 'C.A.T. and Genny' (Cable Avoidance Technology & Signal Generator nicknamed Genny). This was an amazing piece of kit, the Genny was clamped to the gas inlet pipe near the meter, and would then send a signal out through the submerged pipework, then the operator waved the C.A.T. 'to and fro' to try and pick up the signal emanating through the ground.

This would have picked up an older steel gas pipe, but not on plastic. After a few incidents throughout the country, the new replacement plastic pipeline had a metallic 'trace wire' incorporated into the plastic moulding, to try and prevent so many incidents.

Despite me now being an engineer, I fell into the realms of apprentice mode/admiration of the skilled engineers that were before me, and I asked "what would happen if that gas had lit?"

They both turned to me, and Mr. Fleet said in a very calm voice

"Well my boy, you're looking at a 100ft flame, with a 20ft lift off (where the pressure is too great to ignite), like a big 'Bunsen burner' sometimes it's better to be lit, than release it into the wild, thankfully this stuff rises quite quick so unless you're Bertha in her van on top of it, you'll be ok".

We all sniggered, as I stood in awe of his knowledge, I was like a sponge for these facts, and absorbed them, hence the reason why this book is being compiled, along with a few others in the pipeline (see what I did there?).

They'd seen some years of graft, they knew the 'beast', and trust me, gas is a chemical, but you learn it's a dangerous beast too. That we, as engineers need to understand it's characteristics, that NO college can ever teach you. It's only when you see how it behaves in real life...and only then you learn that we can keep this beast tamed.

Note – Sadly, as time has ticked on, we're not getting any younger, and the legends of BG that I knew are slowly fading into the history books, this book is not only of my life, but a memorial of the people that I met, and had a lasting impact in my memory.

R.I.P. to Mr. Fleet, you were a legend in our eyes, and always will be.

CHAPTER TWENTY
A 'break' from the old routine

I don't mention much about my life out of BG in this book, and the reason for this is because it's about my working life, not my own life. Although this particular chapter in my life could've changed my young life, and this is why I am compelled to add this.

Christmas Day 1990

I leave the house I am renting with my mate 'Pierre' and his girlfriend 'Chin' (this will be explained in my next book) dressed in my finest attire, suit, shirt and tie. It's Christmas Day, and I'm hoping to impress my girlfriend's parents, and grandparents by being in my best 'clobber'.

It was a cold morning, with a very light blue clear sky (you notice this as you get older), Jack Frost had been very busy in the night, and had laid a thick layer of his magical frozen dust over everything outside.

I was a witness to this, as I scraped the ice from the windscreen and windows with a cassette case* before I got into my car, a Ford Sierra 1.6L (I traded in my Mk1 VW Golf, as it had electrical issues, and the insurance was pricey).

I left Cogges Hill Road, music playing at a volume my young ears could cope with. As I reached the brow of Oxford Hill heading toward South Leigh, the music started to play in a different tone, the tape had decided to 'chew up', and Mick Hucknall's voice took a drunken turn/tone whilst singing Stars.

I looked down at the stereo to see what was going on, I looked up,

I looked down again, I looked up to see a shimmer on the road... black ice!

I never touched the brakes, but I put it down a gear. The car started spinning, I couldn't regain control. I saw the grass verge, the road, the bridge, the grass verge, the road, and then...

I hit the bridge side on.

I woke up in my car, covered in cubes of glass from my window. I could feel warm liquid running down my neck and back, I touched my head and looked at my fingers, it was blood.

Then the pain kicked in, it was absolutely excruciating my entire right side was throbbing, and my gear stick (for the car!) was between my legs, clearly where my car had been crumpled.

I was sat there for quite some time, and then a glimmer of hope, a car stopped opposite me, I waved at the occupants, and they just drove off. Not long after a woman came running along with her son, who was carrying a blanket. She was carrying a phone, and said "Don't worry, you'll be fine, we've called an ambulance".

I woke to the sound of the ambulance driver saying "we need the fire brigade; we can't get him out" ...

I woke to a different voice "Don't worry my boy, we're going to get you out" it was a fireman. They began to cut my car up, they cut the pillars of the windscreen, whilst covering my face, then they peeled the roof back (just like you would to get a pilchard out of its tin, although mine was blood not ketchup).

I had a stretcher placed behind me, and then they pulled me out of the wreckage. It felt like someone was running a thousand razor blades up and down my back and pelvis, I cried out in pain, and passed out.

I woke up in the hospital as I was being taken through to be X-Rayed, I had a neck brace on which was standard practice in a Road Traffic Accident (RTA), and they couldn't understand what the two circles were that were in my head, until one of them looked to reveal my earrings, the collar was hiding them!

I apparently had a lucky escape, I'd broken my pelvis in two places, and all of the ribs down my right-hand side, oh, and to top it off, I had a knock to the head (that'll explain a few things!) in the form of a fractured skull.

I spent a few weeks in the hospital recovering, the beautiful nurses were amazing, but were nowhere to be seen during my bed bath time, I had a very elderly nurse doing that, and it was a few months later I realised why.

Moving forward a few months, I was back at work, and fighting fit. I knocked on the front door of this one particular house in Dark Lane, in Witney, and it was soon answered by a gentleman.

"Good afternoon Sir, British Gas, I'm here to service your boiler" I said, and as I did, I noticed the colour drain from his face, he walked away saying "come in, it's this way".

I followed him through to the kitchen, where he perched on a stool, still quite pale, I asked "Are you ok sir, do you need a glass of water?"

He replied "Did you have a car accident on Christmas Day?"

I was completely stumped by this man's knowledge, and replied "yes, but how do you know that?"

"Because I was one of the firemen that helped cut you out, I spoke to you. I'm sorry, but we didn't think you would make it"

My emotions were overwhelmed, this man, this wonderful human being, this true gentleman had saved my life (along with his colleagues, and ALL of the others, the ambulance crew, the doctors, nurses, radiologists etc) I thanked him, hugged him and shook his hand as I left.

Roll on **22** years, I was self-employed, and was asked by a manager of a well-known letting agents in Oxford, to survey for a heating system to be installed in a house that he had just purchased.

"Yes of course I can" I said.

"Excellent Sparta (my nickname due to my company logo), when do you think you can make it?".

"After work today?" I said, noting that this man had passed me a lot of work, I needed to help as best I could.

"Wow, ok, that's great! Although I won't be there, but my Fiancée will, is that ok?".

"Yes, that's fine" I replied, and he gave me the address.

A few hours later I arrived at the property, I knocked on the door, and one of the most beautiful women I had ever seen appeared before me. She was truly stunning.

"Hey Steve, come in, would you like a cup of tea?"

"Yes please, would it be ok to carry on surveying?" I enquired.

"Please do, I'll call you when it's ready" she replied.

While I was measuring the rooms, I heard the door knock, then another voice downstairs. I finished measuring, just as she called up to say my cuppa was ready. I walked into the kitchen to see a man sat with his back to me, and the young lady introduced me to him, as he turned.

We both smiled, it was the very same man who had saved my life as a fireman all those years ago, he stood up, and we shook hands.

"Mr. Gasman" he said, grinning.

"Mr. Fireman, my hero!" I said, grinning too.

"How do you know my dad, Steve?"

"He saved my life my flower" I replied "he's my hero".

I said my goodbyes, and left.

This man who saved my life is called **Steve Fletcher**.

He repairs clocks and watches too, in his shop in my old Shire. You may also know him from the BBC show '**The Repair Shop**', where he, and many others change people's lives with their wonderful skill sets.

They truly are heroes without capes...and Steve...

You'll ALWAYS be my hero.

Thank you.

*Target audience right there, we used to have cassette tapes to play music in our cars, and on our stereos. Type into your search engine TDK90/Kenwood/Technics.

**I kick myself every day having traded in a MK1 golf... for a Ford Sierra?! My only excuse was I was young and dumb!

CHAPTER TWENTY-ONE

Miss Scarlet

It was half way through a warm summer morning as I drove onto the Deer Park estate in Witney, a relatively new estate that was slowly becoming established as part of the town. As a true 'Witneyite', I knew this piece of land as fields before houses, where my grandad and I often flew a kite. Also, in the latter years was a perfect exit for my mates and I, scrumping raspberries from a garden backing onto the fields from Smith's estate, we ate so many one particular time, that we were sick as pigs, and I personally didn't eat any for about 30 years after that.

Anyhow, digression over for the moment, on this particular morning I was due to service a gas fire. I drove slowly into the cul de sac, I noticed the house on the corner was under repair with scaffold surrounding it, like an iron prison, and recalled rumours that this was due to it being struck by lightning a few weeks previous, additional rumours were of the plaster being blown off the walls as the charge travelled down the aerial cable, and exploding the television.

Even more additional rumours, that the house was so full of static electricity that everyone in the house had hair that stood on end for days, including the Persian cat and couldn't fit through its cat flap.

Digression over...

I arrived at the property, gathered my equipment and rang the doorbell, smiling as a lady with long dark curly hair, bright green eyes, and a flowery summer dress answered "good morning, Mr. Gasman, are you hear to service my fire?"

She was so beautiful that I was speechless for a few moments, I was sent back to my school days, to my English lessons, a schoolboy crush with the beautiful English teacher Mrs. Newport.

If she asked you a question, you were guaranteed to completely 'fluff it up' and look like a buffoon as you were dying of embarrassment. Not one of us teenage boys misbehaved in her class, we were hypnotised by her beauty, but also with the books that we all shared together...

Cider with Rosie... 'Z' for Zachariah... Jonathan Livingston Seagull. To this day, 36 years later, the memories are as clear as they were then, of those books, and those sunny days in the classroom, with her flowing dress, blonde curly hair, crystal blue eyes.

Digression over...

"Good morning, yes, I 'm here to service the fire" I said (now I was back in the land of reality).

"Well, you better come in then Mr. Gasman, would you like a cup of tea?" she said, her soft voice floating on the air like a fine scented rose, I floated in behind her answering "yes please, milk with two sugars", she vanished into the kitchen, as I landed gently on the carpet in front of the gas fire.

I did the usual sequence and laid my dust sheet down, tool roll open, and Henry vacuum cleaner (Murley) plugged in. In front of me was a very common gas fire of the time, a Valor Unigas Homeflame, made to look like a real fire by putting ceramic logs on top of a gas burner, but behind a glass screen, and enclosed in a brass and bronze frontage that made it all look very regal.

It looked lovely when it was initially installed, but after 1-2 years of use, due to the products of combustion the glass would turn a 'milky' colour, so the flames could no longer be visible, great idea to keep the pennies rolling in, as the only way to resolve it would be to get a gas engineer round to service it, and to remove the glass for cleaning.

The usual course of action would be, as you cleaned the rest of the fire, and checked the chimney catchment space (the bottom of the chimney that was behind the fire), the customer would take the glass off and clean it with warm soapy water.

This day was no different, the customer and I exchanged objects, my cup of tea, for her gas fire glass. She ventured off as I placed my tea on a coaster on the table. I removed the outer casing, cleaned it with my faithful paint brush and Henry's assistance, placed it on the dust sheet, cleaned the fire, after removing and cleaning each individual log, and placed it behind me.

I was about to peel the tape from the 'enclosure plate' thus revealing the chimney, when the lady sailed into the room like a beautiful ship with floral sails, in her hands was a pristine piece of glass from the fire.

I turned to greet her, and take the valuable cargo from her beautiful hands, my eyes concentrating more on her than the upright gas fire wobbling on its flimsy little feet.

My concentration broke as the fire began to fall toward the carpet, out of the sanctuary of my dust sheet, I reached over to catch it, grabbing the framework, and pulling it back to an upright position.

What happened next very much happened in slow motion, you'll notice this, as I'm now typing slower.

Pulling my hands away from the fire, I breathed a sigh of relief, and as I leant across to grab my cuppa with my right hand, I noticed blood on my dust sheet.

The customer said "good save!", as I glanced down at my left hand, to see my palm bleeding, I lifted it up to inspect and clenched my fingers, it opened a razor-sharp gash like a mouth which proceeded to spray blood at my face, partially blinded in one eye.

I turned to the lady for assistance spraying her with blood too, she sighed, fell onto the sofa. With my cyclops vision, and holding my injured hand tightly, I ventured into the kitchen, grabbed a tea towel, and wrapped it tightly around my hand (we were taught basic first aid as apprentices too).

I walked back into the living room, as the lady was just 'coming round' I tried to explain that I was off to the hospital, sadly she spotted the blood-soaked tea towel and passed out once more. I mopped my blood from her, and felt awful leaving her in that way, but knew I needed urgent medical assistance at the Minot Injuries Unit (MIU) in Witney Hospital, I pulled her door to, left a note to say where I was, then I jumped in the van and drove about a mile (in 1st gear, as I couldn't change gear!) to the hospital.

What felt like four hours later, I entered the hospital MIU reception, explained my predicament, and was asked to sit and wait to be called, due to the severity of my injury it didn't take long for me to be treated. I led on a bed, a nurse removed the tea towel, and proceeded to inspect my wound.

"Oooh... you'll need a few stitches inside and out of this one, but I'll need to inject you with a local anaesthetic, you'll feel a little prick"

I thought "no more than I do already for leaving the lady on her sofa", that changed as the nurse stuck about four needles into what felt like my soul, the pain was horrendous, but once the medicine had taken effect, I watched as she repaired my hand like a Seamstress/Mortician.

As she sewed, I could see my tendons, some bone, and the 'layers of flesh' covering it. Once repaired, it was bandaged, and I was released into the wild. I called my manager (not the infamous legend of Martin Bartlett at this time as he was on secondment to another depot), and was instructed to go home, and that my tools would be collected, along with the job being completed.

Although I knew this was the best plan, I was gutted that I wouldn't get to apologise to the lady for leaving her in such a state, sadly I never did see her again to do so, as my recovery time, and my new found love of a certain young lady from a village of South Leigh had taken over my life.

Therefore, I would just like to thank Valor, and all of the other Manufacturers of gas appliances (especially Worcester) for not ensuring their appliances are 'de-burred' (made with smooth metal edges) in the production process, thus causing injuries to this very day.... oh, and ruining any chance of apologising to my customer.

CHAPTER TWENTY-TWO

Inspector Gadget

I can truly say what makes my job such a fantastic job are the people I have met, and still meet to this day. Some of the people are very eccentric, and some slightly bonkers! This next chapter is proof in the pudding of how boring the world would be if we were all the same, I love it.

On this particular wintry afternoon, I had two jobs in one property, one, to service the gas fire, the second, to resolve a fault on the central heating timer/heating controls.

I arrived outside a red brick Victorian house, with a splendour of wrought iron railings, protecting an immaculately kept garden of privet hedges, to which had probably been trimmed with nail scissors.

It was raining so hard that the rain was horizontal, and so cold, it was like icy needles as it hit any skin that was exposed. I braved this, as I ventured out of the comfort of my warm, dry van, as I gathered my equipment, I silently cursed myself, as the storm found every inch of naked flesh and bit hard.

Thankfully, as I approached the front door, the customer had seen me struggling and was awaiting my arrival with it open, I scuttled in, placing my dust sheet down and shaking myself like a dog to prevent any rain dropping onto the customer's property (as part of my apprenticeship training, care of the customer's property was paramount...you'll see this in my next book).

"Bloody awful weather out there old bean, what say you?" he said, not paying much attention to the customer as I ran in to shelter. I turned to reply, noticing that he had a fine head of silvery grey hair, along with a similar moustache, that wouldn't have looked

out of place on a brigadier general of the army in the 1st world war, or, come to think of it a large bag of steel wool moulded into face furniture.

His attire was that of a college professor, a white overcoat, the top pocket brimming with a multitude of pens that had leaked at some stage, leaving their cry for help in a spattering of partial 'rainbow-coloured' stains at the base of said pocket. He moved in very erratic strides, almost like there was an invisible strobe light going off and tricking my vision, he was in my mind now called Inspector Gadget (IG).

"Yes, it's a bit grotty" I agreed, as I followed him through to the living room, where the gas fire resided. He pointed a long bony finger at it accusingly "there's the beauty!", as I looked at a rather odd connection to the gas fire pipe, I then turned to him about to question what I had just briefly noticed, but thought "leave it for a moment", and the fact he had scurried off like a clockwork robot, and just caught a glimpse of his coat tails as he said "Follow me young man, the programmer needs a look over first!"

I arrived at the bottom of the stairs, a burgundy carpet held captive by brass stair runners in the centre, with beautifully carved balustrades and banister rising to the right, the gent peered over and beckoned me up "up here my good fellow".

I ascended two steps at a time, and met him on the landing in the process of hurling blankets and sheets from their set place in the airing cupboard onto a nearby bed. He apologised for not clearing it prior to my arrival, I nodded, as I gazed at the surroundings, oil paintings of ancestors hung on the wall, all gazing back at me in their ornate golden floral frames.

I moved to the vicinity of the airing cupboard, as he was brushing his crazy professor hair back with his hands into a form that wasn't blinding him, now composed, we both looked into the airing cupboard.

I rubbed my eyes, looking on in disbelief at what was before me.

If you've seen any sci-fi films with space ship control panels, or, video footage of NASA's launch control room, well, this is what was in front of me!

Not happy with a standard clock/programmer to control the hot water and heating, the man had created his very own control system.

It was a carved wooden boxed panel about a 'foot' square (30 cm in new money) festooned with labelled buttons, below tiny red lights flickered. I was blown away by the intricacy and sheer brilliance of the man's workmanship, I was also secretly looking for the 'LAUNCH' button, imagining once pressed, the house would rumble, and then launch into the stratosphere, as the man next to me laughed maniacally, lightly spraying me with his excited saliva as he guffawed.... that button thankfully was nowhere to be seen.

"What seems to be the problem here?" regretting the question, and cursing my brain for allowing my voice to activate before I had chance to stop it (a very common fault with me, as you may have noticed).

"This is the issue" as his fingers moved over the buttons and almost became a blur, the control panel sprang into life, and he continued "the heating doesn't appear to come on, no matter what time I request, and the room thermostat is turned up".

The cogs of industry began to grind as my diagnostic thought process kicked in, thankfully, it was nothing to do with his home-made launchpad, but a motor burnt out on a 3-way valve.

"It's this that's the issue" pointing to the valve "I'll have to turn the power off to the system to change it". The look the man gave me was almost like I was telling him I would have to imprison his entire family unless he paid me a hearty ransom, it was of pure terror.

"Why do you have to turn the power off?" he enquired.

I wanted to say "so I don't touch cloth like the last time I touched a live wire", thankfully my brain was still in snooze mode, so didn't let that one out before I politely said "because I need to disconnect 5 wires in the wiring centre, and I don't want to stop my heart" letting out a little chuckle.

Beads of sweat appeared on the man's forehead, as he let out a nervous laugh, and twirled his moustache between his thumb and forefinger "This means I'm going to have to re-programme my timing module, as it has no backup power reserve".

I truly felt an air of sadness for the man as I watched him kill the power to his invention, as the lights faded "I'll pop to my van and get the replacement motor, won't be a sec" I said, and left the man standing in the same statuesque pose he had, as he killed the power.

I descended the stairs to be met midway by Mrs.Gadget, a rather rotund lady with dark curly hair, rosy cheeks, and dressed in a daffodil patterned dress, with a rose print apron, she was like a mobile kaleidoscope of colour "would you like a cup of tea?" she asked, her voice very soft, unlike her husband, who not only had a strange walk, his voice was slightly screechy, not far from 'fingernails down a blackboard' tone.

Being a young man of the 90's with the new age of 'Love & Peace' in the rave scene, I along with many other friends had tried certain drugs, L.S.D. was one of them, it was a hallucinogenic drug, played tricks with your mind, and you had to be in a happy place, with good friends. This house was like that but without dropping a tab!

I blinked "Yes please, milk and two sugars thank you", she nodded and ascended past me. I glanced in at the gas fire on my way out of the front door, shaking my head, as I grabbed my coat.

The rain had subsided for a moment, that moment being, as soon as I stepped out from the shelter of the house and had one foot on the driveway the deluge began once more. Cursing as I opened the back of the van, and grabbed the motor, pocketing it, I made a run for the house, shaking myself once more as I peeled my coat off.

I could hear the distant mumble of conversation of the occupants behind a door in the hall, as I grabbed my tool roll and dust sheet, and ran up the stairs to my destination.

The motor was a cinch to change, and the power was turned on in no time, I was met by a whirring of electricity coursing through the control centre, and a mass of flashing lights.

I ventured downstairs and rapped on the kitchen door before entering, I was met by a smell of sweetness, and before me was a plethora of cakes iced, and of different sizes, the lady was carrying out a taster of one, as the husband watched in awe at the sheer size of the slice that was being devoured.

"All done" I said, interrupting the feast, and catching the lady unaware, trying to hide her embarrassment she turned to hide her bulging cheeks and started to cough and splutter. I glanced at the man, who was sipping his tea, he put his cup down and said "excellent, I'll go and start the reprogramming process, it should only take 45 minutes".

In the meantime, his wife was shuddering, and her spluttering and coughing had accelerated in sound, leading to a crumb eruption from her mouth, she was almost like a floral volcano, as she turned with bloodshot eyes, erupting not so much crumbs now, more like small slices of cake that could feed a child.

He could tell by my look that him leaving the room was not a good idea, and 'strobe lighted' over to his beautiful behemoth, placing a direct strike on her back with the flat of his hand.

A shower of cake flew from her 'cakehole' and covered the contents of the W.I. cake stand she had been preparing, leaving her gasping for air, as crumbs floated down the trails of snot from her nostrils. She waved a hand to gesture us both out of the kitchen, as she reached for a glass of water nearby, I was the first to exit the scene, followed very quickly by IG.

Mopping his brow with a hanky, he nervously chuckled stating that "Mrs.G is an expert cake maker, and taster for the W.I. and has won many awards" then changed course "off to the gas fire!" he piped, and strode off like an arthritic grasshopper into the front room, where I followed, to be met by him sprawled across a chais longue padding his forehead with said hanky.

"Sorry young man, but Mrs.G sometimes gets in a state with her baking, and I feel I need to vacate the area" he said as he slowly sat up. I nodded, as we both looked toward the gas fire, he stammered "the fire needs a service, it's been in about five years, and it's never been looked at, I trust you'll ensure it's safe for use?"

I looked down at the 'pipe' connecting the fire to the supply, and followed the route through to the meter under the stairs, the gas fire was connected to the gas meter supply with a garden hose, and two 'jubilee' clips. Its route was under the carpet, hugging the skirting board, but left a slight mound in the carpet leading through the hallway, to the understairs cupboard.

Yes folks, this wasn't right, no professional gas engineer would ever do this (and admit it), "you do realise that's a garden hose connecting your fire to the gas meter under your stairs sir?"

"Oh yes, and it's done a sterling job, although Mrs. G always complains when she vacuum's the hallway it jars on the mound", I pondered his reply, and decided in the moment of madness at my trip into 'Wonderland' to test the gas supply for leaks, I ventured to the van and back, ignoring the rain.

The test at the meter proved 'sound' meaning no leaks throughout the property on ANY of the gas pipework, I was amazed, but not an idiot.

This was illegal pipework, classed as an Immediately Dangerous situation, and had to be resolved. I advised IG of this, and he started to enquire why it needed to be made safe, until the radio was switched off in the kitchen, then IG immediately changed his persona, and said "quickly resolve it, and I'll sign anywhere I need to!"

I realised this was an early warning siren for the movement of Mrs.G, I capped the pipe off, tested for leaks, and filled the paperwork out, he signed and hid the paperwork...just as the kitchen door handle rattled.

Mrs.G entered the hallway, and handed me a cake from her W.I. stall, apologising for her choking incident, I told her there was no need to apologise, or, to give me one of her finely made (and saliva covered) cakes.

She insisted and handed me the cake, as I handed over the paperwork for the repair to the heating, it was like a 'bum' deal, I'd made their house safe, yet they were endangering my life with the 'spittle' cake.

I bid farewell, as Mrs. G was waving a tea towel, and IG was mopping his brow with his hanky. I drove away from the property, and not long after, the cake was ejected into a field, where I knew nature wouldn't be as fussy as me.

CHAPTER TWENTY-THREE

What a Hoot!

From a young age, a gas engineer works in various habitats, mainly inside the dwelling of his fellow shaved primates, usually in the dark recesses i.e., roof spaces and cellars, but also outside too. This can sometimes lead to being at one with nature, or being the nemesis of each other, and these following chapters reveal a small section of this experience. Therefore, I feel it only fair but to warn you that the chapters involve the following:

Wasps, mice & Birds (numerous species), to which I feel I have a spiritual link with...not wasps...they're 'stripey stingy bastards' who hate everything! Amazing how such a small thing can invoke fear into the majority of the animal kingdom, including a group of bodybuilders sharing a protein shake on a park bench, that could usually crush your car with their bare hands in seconds, would run like fairies away from a wasp.

Moving away from the 'stripey stingy bastards' to the feathered beauties...

BG wouldn't charge customers for the release of birds from behind their fires, as they had a 'gentleman's agreement' setup with the R.S.P.B. (Royal Society for the Protection of Birds), that they too cared for all wildlife, including birds.

The chapter starts with firstly, changing from my Maestro van G881 UOW, to a Ford Transit F37 OTR, this was a very moving moment for me, as sadly we'd lost 'Chad' out of our family a few months previous to this. I was tasked to clean the van out as an apprentice, and now, as an engineer, it would be my van. Chad, it was an honour to have your van, to this day it still is an honour.

Secondly, me receiving a call of 'bird behind fire' on my CB, to save a very long-winded description, I'll bullet point the typical scenario of this quite common occurrence (less so nowadays due to lack of gas fires, or that 'cowls' had been fitted to prevent bird entry). Here is a typical scenario:

Autumn/Winter seasons...

- The customer turns fire on in morning to warm up, a feathered friend is perched on the chimney benefiting from the warmth rising up, also to kill mites in their feathers (allegedly).
- The bird is overcome by fumes from the fire, and plummets down the chimney, sustaining no damage as it's 'off its beak' with mild Carbon Monoxide poisoning so is as limp as a rotting lettuce leaf.
- The customer turns the fire off, and goes off to work, or...another wonderful adventure.
- The bird wakes after breathing fresh air from the base of the chimney, as it's landed in a space past the fire flue/outlet.
- The customer returns home, turns the fire on, only to be met with a frantic flapping of wings and squawking, to which they turn the fire off, and phone the gas emergency number.

It was an early Autumnal evening when I arrived at the property in the glorious realms of Chipping Norton, the home of the towns Tweed Mill, but more importantly, Mossy, Turv, Wedge & Ferret (the apprentice) ...my fellow colleagues.

I rapped on the door knocker of a semi-detached pebble dashed house, a rusting car in the drive, with moss and lichen becoming its camouflage cloak, slowly allowing it to blend in with the fading life of orange, red, yellow and brown leaves of its surrounding shrubs and trees, equally unkempt.

A light appeared from the darkness of the frosted glass of the front door, followed by a dark figure ambling toward it, an outside light came on, reducing my vision by 90%, I squinted and quietly cursed for being temporarily blinded.

A key turned in the lock and the door opened revealing a short, portly, bespectacled man, with hands that were out of proportion to his body, it was like a scene from The Kenny Everett Show – Brotherly Love sketch (google it, but make sure you include Kenny Everett in the search), and his glasses were so strong I could see bacteria dancing on his eyeballs (ok, maybe slightly exaggerated... you may find I do this throughout my book...a bit).

Here was Mr. Mole.

My silent cursing fizzled out as soon as I saw this man, Mr. Mole beckoned me in, I greeted him, and shook his large hand, my hand being engulfed by his like a minnow being eaten by a whale (thankfully without the bone crusher mentality of Steph).

"Thank goodness you're here mate, I'm not sure what's behind the fire but it doesn't sound too happy!" said Mr. M, I was a little taken aback by his greeting, as the term 'mate' was used mainly by my younger generation, I replied "Ok mate, let's get this sorted then" which seemed the correct response as I followed him into his lounge.

This was a very spacious room, very minimalist, consisting of two sets of patio doors, highly polished parkay flooring, the walls were wallpapered with 60's style psychedelic wavy lines.

The contents consisted of two white arm chairs, a coffee table to match the flooring, a sheepskin rug in front of the fireplace, a standard lamp, a couple of pot plants, and a stereo stack system including a record player, this was quietly playing the absolutely fantastic classic 'Jeff Wayne's War of the Worlds' in the background.

Richard Burton describing the affairs of the last years of the 19th century was interrupted by a squawk from the fireplace, that definitely wasn't your usual pigeon I thought. I advised Mr. M. that the procedure involved me covering the fire surround with a dust sheet, disconnecting the gas fire and removing it, and then capturing said bird, and releasing it into the wild, to which he must let me solely be in control as to evade any undue stress of an already stressed bird.

After carrying out the above preparation, I decided I needed another dust sheet for the operation, and explained to Mr. M that under no circumstances was he to get involved with this, to which he agreed.

I ventured out to my van, and on my return as I walked into the hallway, I heard a different kind of squawk, this wasn't a bird, but Mr. M who had chosen to ignore my instructions, and carry out his own rescue operation.

I walked into the room to see Mr. M clutching his hand, blood dripping onto his sheepskin rug, he wailed "It's a monster in there!" as he scuttled off, I asked if he needed assistance, he shouted "no, I think I've learnt my lesson, leave it to the professionals" his voice ebbing away as he disappeared to clean his wound.

I opened one set of curtains, along with the now revealed patio doors, and turned on the outside lights. Just as Justin Hayward was singing 'Forever Autumn', I placed the dust sheet down on the hearth, I donned my gauntlets, and gently slid my hand into the chimney breast. I could feel something pecking frantically at my protected fingers, and unlike Mr. M, I had a chance to capture the bird without injury.

I reached down, and gently took hold of what felt like legs, the pecking continued, along with the background of 'Forever Autumn'... "cos you're not here" playing in the background. I pulled my hand out, revealing the entrapped bird…

I couldn't believe my eyes, being used to releasing pigeons, jackdaws, blackbirds, this was the elite…

Before me was a young Barn Owl, it immediately calmed down as it was brought out into the room, it stopped flapping & pecking. And for a beautiful brief moment it looked at me, and I looked at it, as the music played in the background.

"You have nothing to fear from me my friend" I said softly, as I walked over to the standard lamp, the owl sat on my gauntlet, as I turned off the lamp, I whispered "time for you to see your family" and walked to the open patio door, the only light was outside now, I opened my hand…

The beautiful and majestic bird left my hand, and silently flew out through the patio door, as the crazy vicar Nathaniel kicked off on the record. A truly mesmerising moment, only for a few seconds, but still stays to me this day.

I tested the chimney with a smoke bomb to ensure it wasn't blocked, it wasn't, so I connected the gas fire and carried out the required tests to ensure it was safe, it was.

I gathered my tools and dust sheets and walked into the hallway, to be met by Mr. M, sporting a rather over the top bandage dressing to his minor injury, looking more like a boxer, he waved as I advised him to get a builder to attach chicken wire to the top of his chimney pot, otherwise he would be charged for the next callout.

This wasn't entirely true, but I was, and still do care for our wildlife, so I always advised a mesh needed to be fitted to a chimney pot.

As I left Chipping Norton and drove back to Witney through the beautiful winding roads, I was met by a Barn Owl flying briefly alongside me before a tiny hamlet of Spelsbury, then flying off into the darkness.

I'd like to think that this was the same owl, giving me a 'flyby'.

I felt at one with nature that night, along with many more nights throughout my life.

I always have.

CHAPTER TWENTY-FOUR

Tranquil Retreat

It was a scorching hot summer's day as I sat in my van in the beautiful town of Woodstock, steeped in history, mainly linked to Sir Winston Churchill who resided at Blenheim Palace. My windows were down in the van (that was the air con of the day), Simon Mayo was on Radio 1 playing another glorious hit by A-Ha, as I began to tuck into my ham, cheese & coleslaw bap from 'Kay's Pantry' (a shop that was part of the garage in Long Hanborough, sadly, no longer there).

A call came through on my now newly upgraded handset, a 'Marconi' early version of a mobile phone (nobody knew it would eventually be the demise of society).

The handset 'bleeped', I picked it up to hear the wondrous voice of Elaine, the heart-throb to all emergency engineers, with no clue how she looked, it mattered not, her voice was soothing at 3am as you called in to report you were going home. We all had our own idea how Elaine looked in our minds eye, and that's all that mattered.

"Spike, it's Elaine are you receiving? Over" The parameters had changed regarding our new handsets, unlike our old ones, these ones were designated numbers to an individual. If only this was available a few months earlier as I remembered, the drunken lady hostage scenario radio 'banter'!

"Hi Elaine, receiving, over" I replied.

"We have reports of a water leak on the heating pipes in the gate keeper's cottage of Blenheim Palace, please investigate, over"

"Received, will do. Over and out" I started the van, and made my way to the entrance, a few seconds later explaining my reasons to enter the grounds, I was on my way to the water leak.

I took a gentle drive through the grounds of this truly historical and breath-taking place, admiring the shimmer of the lake passing between the bridge leading upto a monument as I crossed it, spotting young lovers rowing a boat and laughing together... this is how life should be I thought, and still do.

I arrived at the cottage to be met by the gate keeper, a short, stocky uniformed chap with a peaked cap, round spectacles and a small pencil lined moustache, he was Mr. Flynn (like Errol but shorter....so I called him Er).

I was about to exit my van to greet him, but a German Shepherd dog the size of a bear appeared from behind a perfectly trimmed privet hedge put pay to that! (I nearly repeated a similar episode of 'brown trouser' antics in a previous episode, in the same of town too). I closed my door just in time to have the paws stop me from raising my window, as a huge tongue licked my arm as I cowered.

I could hear muffled laughter, as the 'Hound of the Baskervilles' stunt double lapped at my skin, 'Er' called the hound away...

"Poppy...heel!", the dog immediately left, and sat next to him astonished, I enquired, as I regained my composure, exiting my van "Poppy? That's a different name for a dog of that size".

"The wife's favourite flower, so she named the dog the same" he said, completely unmoved by my traumatic moment. "You're here for the water leak? The door's open, and the stain is in the lounge. The place is empty as we moved out yesterday" ... as he tossed me the keys, catching them, he requested I take them back to the office, I nodded accordingly as he walked off with 'Poppy' by his side.

I watched them as they walked over the brow of a nearby pathway, then I walked to the cottage. It was a single storey cottage, a bungalow in an estate agent's property description. I opened the door, walking into a small whitewashed entrance hall with a flagstone floor, two aged braced doors, one to my left, one to my front, before me.

I opened the left door and entered into an empty room, apart from an umbrella stand, with a solitary black umbrella sporting a bamboo handle.

I walked in, the door closed behind me, a replica of the door directly next to this, opening it, at a glance, it was a small broom cupboard. Examining the ceiling as I ventured around the barren, curtainless, whitewashed room, the sun was gleaming through the lead lined windows, as I noticed a slight brown blemish to a part of the ceiling.

I had noticed that the heating pipes were nowhere in this vicinity, and as I approached the blemish, I could hear a scratching sound.

From previous experience I assumed it was a mouse creating this noise, so thought I'd test this by tapping the ceiling, thus scaring said rodent across the ceiling, and reporting back to the main office.

Surprise was the key to this operation, so no time to go to my van to grab a screwdriver/piece of pipe to get the furry critter moving, so I grabbed the brolly, and gently tapped the blemish with the point.

At this point, in this moment of time, on this day, in this year...

Hell was unleashed (I'm not religious, but this description I imagine is Hell).

As the point hit the blemish, a tennis ball hole appeared... along with a lot of very angry wasps!

Without thinking, I opened the brolly, threw it up in the air, and thankfully exited the room via the 'correct' door, as I saw the swarm attacking the brolly out of the corner of my eye.

I ran blindly to the sanctuary of my van, windows were wound up in seconds, thankfully with no followers. I started the van, taking a slow drive past the cottage, I could see the windows of the cottage completely covered by wasps, along with swarms of the stripey b@stards outside having a self-provoked frenzy, like a scene from a horror film.

I was still shuddering as I reported back to the office, witnessing three members of staff recoiling in horror at the same time as I described what I had just witnessed. I left as they were sorting out a pest control company and ventured back to my van, reporting back to Elaine of my findings, and couldn't help but notice an electronic shudder from my phone as I mentioned the number of wasps.

As I type this episode, with Guy Tipton's album playing in the background (thanks mate), my hackles are up thinking of the number of stings that could have been administered, if I had chosen the wrong door to run through, probably a good chance of the death of yours truly.

CHAPTER TWENTY-FIVE

No Sirens

In the early hours of a wintry morning (2am to be precise) the phone rang, I awoke from a deep slumber, fumbling around I lifted the receiver "Hello" I croaked, as the pilot light of my brain lit. A voice on the other end said "Hi Spike, we've got an uncontrolled gas leak in Oxford that needs attending, ok to respond?"

In my sleepy mind, I wanted to say "No, it can wait", but the main burner had lit when the word 'uncontrolled' was mentioned, to save you leafing back through this fantastic book and jumping away from this sheer exhilarating moment, an uncontrolled escape meant that the customer had turned the gas off, but could still smell it. This was not a good thing.

I jumped out of bed, threw my uniform on, and within minutes was racing down the A40 with my invisible 'blues & twos' going, in my faithful Transit van.

In my mind I was wondering if this was going to be another prank from a drunken bum prawn that had just crawled out of a night club, stumbled to a payphone (yes, this was before mobile phones...thankfully) and told their mates how hilarious it was to see so many gas engineers turn up and sniff around drains (not literally, as our Gasco seeker machines did that, not our noses).

Side splitting if you were smashed off your titties...maybe. Not so, if you were a sleep deprived gas engineer, that had already responded to four other similar callouts that weekend, and was so tired, that murdering the perpetrator, and burying them in a shallow grave seemed like a good idea...and foxes biting their toes was an added bonus.

This thought immediately changed as I turned into a quiet suburban road, far away from the inebriated muppetry, driving slowly along the road, a line of terraced red brick houses divided by a slim grass verge mirrored my peripheral vision either side, along with an avenue of trees that had long since shed their canopy of leaves.

The dimly lit road concealed the family in their pyjamas until my headlights shone upon them all, their hands raised together in a strange salute to protect their eyes, a mother and father, with two children huddled together by the kerbside.

I pulled up alongside them, jumped out and asked them the usual questions:

i)   Have you turned the gas off at the meter?...Yes
ii)   Where can you smell gas?...Upstairs

I advised them to stay where they were as I carried out a test at their gas meter, sure enough no leaks detected. I ventured into their house, and ran up the stairs. My Gasco seeker ticking gently like a clock on a mantelpiece, I raised the probe upto the ceiling, at this point it went from tick to a continuous tone, as did my heartbeat, as I looked down at the display.

It was showing 1% Gas in Air (in case I've not mentioned this before, the explosive limit of Natural Gas has a range of 5-15% gas in air, and 1% in a house where the gas is turned off meant it was filtering through from next door.

Despite the bitterly cold weather, I opened every window upstairs in the house to reduce the chance of the house exploding, I ventured downstairs, checked the gas readings around the main electric isolation, it was safe, so I killed the power to the house.

I ran to the shuddering family, and asked who lived next door, through chattering teeth from the gent, I decoded it was an elderly lady called Gladys who was quite forgetful.

I needed to act fast, my training kicked in...safeguard life, safeguard property.

Seeing frost almost forming on the family, I broke protocol, and ushered them into the front cab, it was a bit of a squeeze for them. As I started the engine to power the heater on, I pleaded with them not to sound the horn, or fiddle with the phone/radio, as they could die in the explosion that was about to take place.

They all agreed, and the parents restrained their young in their arms in a very, very loving cuddle. Maybe I would apologise later for terrifying them all, but in the meantime, I really did need to prevent an explosion.

I ran over to the house of Gladys, and slipped the extended probe through her letterbox, despite the double entendre, this was a tense moment...

The Gasco seeker read 2%...

I looked through the letterbox to see the gas ring on the cooker was lit...

I looked for any other way of entry, and ran down an alleyway, entering into a shared garden, I gently tried the back door, it was locked, I looked up to see a bedroom window partially open, yet had no means to get there.

My heart and mind were racing, the chances of the entire block of twenty 'gas filled' rooves of these terraced houses exploding was imminent, and now down to my actions of the next few minutes.

I couldn't turn the gas off as the gas meter was inside, so I couldn't turn off the potential bomb. I couldn't knock on the door as she might turn on her bedside lamp causing a spark, and I definitely couldn't try the doorbell!

I ran to the van, opened the door and grabbed the handset, pressed 9 on my handset, it got me through to the emergency services.

"Which service do you require?" said the operator.

"All of them!" I said, and explained my reasoning…

Police – to force entry (although I had that power in these circumstances) clear the roads, and control any crowds.

Fire – to assist in preventing any explosions, if not, dealing with explosions and reducing loss of life.

Ambulance – to attend to any possible injured or traumatised people.

The words I always remember repeating after confirmation of all services on their way was…

"No Sirens, or lights, No Sirens, or lights, No Sirens, or lights"

"Roger, confirmed" was the reply, this stopped my echo.

There was a reason for this, any disturbance, and Gladys could turn her bedside light on, and that split second would change a lot of people's lives forever.

I pressed 1 (code 1 was a critical call, we usually dialled in 4 digits) for my emergency control room, by the tone in my voice they knew this was serious, and carried out my request for a distribution gang to attend. Not to dig down to cut the gas off to prevent a blast, but to turn the gas off that would be fuelling the fire after the explosion.

I placed the handset in its cradle, and considered moving the sleeping family to a safer place, that was swept away as I heard the approach of a lot of vehicles.

I assured the family all would be ok, as reinforcements were here and it would all be over in no time. I knew this wasn't true, but they needed to know this, as hysterical people screaming wasn't what I needed, and more importantly, I didn't want Gladys to hear!

I exited the van, and walked towards the recent arrivals, a fleet of emergency vehicles from all three groups, and a lot of high-ranking people all looking at me for answers. We gathered together as I explained the situation, I was in 'duck mode', calm and collective on the surface, yet beneath the surface it was panic stations.

Time was of the essence due to the nature of the situation, we literally had a few minutes to devise a plan, or there would be the dealings of the aftermath…

An enormous explosion of twenty properties, with adjacent properties caught in the blast…so we're looking at 60 properties…

The figures were flying through my mind, centre of the blast average house containing 2 people, there would be forty fatalities.

Adjacent, eighty with life changing injuries/fatal.

Extended blast radius, another eighty would be life changing, to minor injuries.

All would suffer possible irreversible ear damage due to the shockwave.

The plan was hatched…

It involved a WPC (Woman Police Constable), myself, and a fireman.

WPC 'Brown' was a very svelte, dark-haired lady, of similar height and age to myself, but you never asked a lady her age, especially in uniform, oh and of course, with hundreds of people's lives hanging in the balance.

Fireman 'Dan' was on the other hand, was built to put out fires and rescue anything from anywhere, he was huge! He could probably put out a forest fire by patting the ground a couple of times. Or, rescue someone from a car crash by tearing the doors off, then the roof.

It ran through my mind for a split second as to why we all had to risk our lives, when selfishly, we could just get dan to tear the front door off, and clap to put the cooker out? This of course vanished as fast as it had appeared, down to the fact that Gladys would turn her bedside light on...BOOM!

The team was assembled, and met for their first, and possibly last rescue mission as the ladder was handed to us. No time for formal introductions, as I knew the urgency of the situation, grabbing the ladder I whispered "follow me, it's urgent".

Within seconds we were at the back, narrowly missing the neighbour's greenhouse, and creating an alarm clock for Gladys the time bomb. The ladder was in position, and WPC Brown, myself, and Fireman Dan were at the top of the ladder in seconds, all armed with 'intrinsically' safe torches (torches that wouldn't cause a spark when turned on), we all gazed at the tiny opened window, hearing the snoring from within, this was a good sound.

"What happens if Gladys turns the light on?" came a whispered call from the darkness.

"We'll be fine" I hissed back, knowing full well it would be down to forensics to trace us if she did turn the light on.

As the ladder shook, the next few moments were almost a blur, a mix of so many emotions, adrenaline, auto pilot, and sheer terror. After opening a larger window, WPC Brown entered like a ninja assassin diving on the unsuspecting pensioner.

Gladys released an ear-piercing wail of Banshee proportions, as Dan and I clambered through the window and ran past the wrestling women. I ventured downstairs, jumping the majority of the steps. I could hear Dan opening the windows above me, and Gladys the 'air raid' siren still wailing.

I reached the cooker, turned off the unlit grill, and the lit hotplate ring in one fell swoop, and within another moment I was in the understairs cupboard to turn the gas off.

Knowing the explosive limits of gas, I knew we were safe, as the house was in darkness, and we were all in one piece. I ventured out of the tiny cupboard, opening the rest of the windows downstairs, along with the front door.

I was confronted by a lot of ghostly white faces from all of the emergency services, all of them letting off a quiet sigh of relief as I could see a joint rising of steam from them all as they exhaled.

WPC Brown, a now 'non wailing' Gladys, and Fireman Dan, appeared at the bottom of the stairs. The reason for Gladys no longer wailing was because she was in the arms of Dan, and was now drooling over the uniformed hunk, gently stroking his chiselled jawline and mumbling incoherent but loving noises.

We all walked outside, all keeping relatively quiet, as my colleagues were monitoring gas levels in other properties to ensure there would be no chance of any explosive issues.

As Gladys was carried into an ambulance by Dan, a few firemen walked over, handing him a cup of something warm as he exited the vehicle.

WPC Brown was escorted to a riot van, where she was given a cuppa, and surrounded by her clan patting her on the back.

I had my 'on call manager' from BG patting me on the back saying "your first evacuation eh my boy? You did a good job" as he handed me a cuppa, a few of the other engineers patted my back, and we chinked our cups and drank in unison.

That night, as a young gas engineer, I saw the camaraderie of every emergency service, how they all cared for their own, but it wasn't just that, we all cared for each other. This made me feel complete, after my other experiences as an emergency engineer, I was part of a family...

An intact family at that! As it wasn't just the 20 houses of sleeping people, it was the impact of these properties exploding on the surrounding area. It would have been over 100 properties, with untold casualties (I found this out later after an incident briefing).

CHAPTER TWENTY-SIX
Smelly Tank

To this day, this particular event makes me feel a bit queasy, and I've seen a LOT of nasty things, so I'll not spoil the surprise.

*Please, if you have a sensitive stomach, just crawl into a bin bag, then get into your shower/bath/car wash and read on...with a bowl ready.

It was a fresh summer morning, skies were blue, and even at 7.30 in the morning, it was warm enough to break into a sweat. There was no 'air con' in those days, apart from the window, and travelling at speed which allowed for a cooling breeze to enter the van.

I was called out to the city of dreaming spires (Oxford), where many famous people had spent their younger years studying, and finding their hidden talents, that would one day make them famous throughout the world. Einstein, JRR Tolkien (& Spike... hopefully) ... to name but a few, of many.

However, on this occasion, sadly this wasn't a dream, and I was not that blessed with their 'grey matter'.

My call was to attend to 'smelly water' at a house in the city centre? When questioning the control room of this description, the reply was "they've got smelly water, that's all we know".

As I sat in the usual queue along the Botley Road sweating profusely, as no air through van windows meant...sauna! I thought for a brief moment what 'smelly water' could mean, this lasted only a few seconds as my thoughts were broken by the sound of car horns, and shouting.

I craned my neck to see where the noise was coming from, and gazed upon a disgruntled bearded man wearing an oversized top hat covered in badges, he was mouthing some muffled obscenity whilst moving a tricycle with buckled wheels from the road to the designated cycle path, then onto the path.

He was followed by a burly builder, a bronzed behemoth, donning a sun/sweat bleached vest and shorts gesticulating his innocence by pointing to the road, his van, and the tricycle.

As the traffic began to move on, my mind did too, as The Prodigy 'Firestarter' played on the radio, and it wasn't long before my journey and this epic song was over, as I parked up outside the customers house enjoying the last of that infamous song, and my fag.

As I closed the door on the back of my van, tool roll and dust sheet in hand, I was greeted by a man and woman at their open front door, and their welcoming didn't stop there. I was invited into the house, and was ushered into a large dining room, flowery wallpaper covered the walls, with matching flowery patterned curtains, and it didn't stop there...the carpet was flowery, along with the table cloth covering the dining table, the cushions on the chairs, yes, you guessed it...flowery!

I began to wonder if these people were bees in a previous life? That was quickly interrupted by a flowery tea cosy being removed, and a flowery cup being filled with a 'gasman's nectar'...tea. As I thanked the lady as she passed me the cup, I took a sip as they began their explanation of their plight.

They explained in chronological order the first detection of the strange smell emanating from their taps, but oddly only upstairs. As they were describing it, they were taking it in turns per sentence, almost like they had rehearsed it. I felt like I was part of a verbal tennis match, craning my neck left, then right, and in hindsight, I should have asked them to stand together, in front of me.

From what I could piece together from their joint story was I needed to resolve this issue on this visit, as Mr & Mrs Bee (newly christened by yours truly) clearly were very concerned, and had gradually worsened over the last 3 months.

They escorted me upstairs to the family bathroom, before I had chance to investigate Mrs Bee took centre stage, and I watched the play unfold along with Mr. Bee. The hot water tap on the basin was opened, as Mrs. Bee held her toothbrush in her hand, and explained that brushing their teeth in the hot water it tasted very strange, and bathing was even worse. I enquired why they used the hot tap to brush their teeth, as most people use cold? Mr. Bee stated that they'd always 'washed' their teeth in hot water, this reply stopped me from enquiring any further, practical assessment was now required.

I requested they leave me to investigate on my own in the roof space, as I needed full concentration, with no distractions (and so I could escape from what seemed madness too), to which they agreed, and would stand vigil at the base of the ladder, as Mr. Bee lowered the roof space hatch, and ladder.

I turned the basin hot tap on, and sure enough, it emitted a strange aroma, not of flowers, but of something that would bring a tear to a glass eye. I tried the cold tap; it had the same pungent smell. I moved to the bath tap/shower and it too was disgusting, I needed to nip this in the bud, at source.

I grabbed my headtorch from my pocket, turned it on, and ventured into the roof space as Mr & Mrs. Bee stood nearby. The heat hit me as I stepped onto a small platform, as the sun was at its highest and warmest point in the sky, beating down onto a vast amount of roof tiles, turning the roof space into a kiln (that heat is unbearable, and it never changes in 35 years, it's still awful, especially wringing your boxer shorts out after sitting in the customers tank to cool down...joking! Sort of...I was usually naked...I'm definitely joking).

As my light scanned the darkness in search of the water storage tank, I noticed the loft insulation was nowhere to be seen as it was a mass of moving darkness, and as my light hit it, it erupted. I was hit by a swarm of flies, thankfully I had my mouth closed as they hit me at speed, attracted by the brightness of my light, knowing they were harmless (unlike the Blenheim cottage episode), I turned the light off, and they immediately left the roof space to seek freedom via the light from the opening.

I cannot apologise enough to Mr & Mrs. Bee to this very day for the release of sheer horror that I unleashed on them, to save my own scrawny arse. I heard a mass of screams from below, and an exodus of two panic-stricken people vaulting down the stairs, and fighting over each other to evade the flying foes.

I turned my light on, and was met with a couple of straggler flies, but nothing to worry about. I made my way over to the 50-gallon water storage tank, as I approached the tank, there was nothing covering it, not even a board, meaning the water was open to everything in the roof space, and the smell was very pungent, and matched that from the taps.

*Are you sitting comfortably?

My light moved over to the open water in the tank, and revealed a large round object, as I approached closer, I could see it was feathered. It turned out to be a very bloated dead pigeon, that had fancied a dip, but couldn't get out. This is what Mr & Mrs Bee (& other family members) had been 'washing' their teeth, washing their hands, showering and bathing in for a few months.

I heard Mr. Bee call from below "We had a plague of flies hit us; are you ok up there?".

"I've found the problem, have you got a couple of bin bags?" I replied.

"Yes of course" said Mr. Bee "what was the problem?"

I moved to the opening, to see them both looking very flustered, this was about to change.

"It's a dead pigeon sir, and I need to remove it"

The colour drained from their faces, and Mr. Bee started 'retching' uncontrollably, this set Mrs. Bee off, and she began to match the timing of the 'retch', I couldn't help but grin as they scurried off to the bathroom together.

A few moments later, they appeared with more colour in their cheeks, but with blood shot watery eyes, and a couple of bags were placed in my hand, and I ventured back to my decaying find. As I touched the 'feathered ball' to grab and bag it, it disintegrated, turning the entire 50-gallon tank into pigeon soup.

The smell from that hit the back of my nose, and I had no warning sign, I instantly puked into the tank, turning it from pigeon, to minestrone. I composed myself, leaving the bags in the tank.

My job was now complete.

Why you may ask?

BG didn't cover this type of plumbing under the customer's contract. To resolve this issue completely, the tank and hot water cylinder needed replacing, as no cleaning/flushing would ever remove all of the pigeon, or bacteria caused by the heating of the pigeons remains inside the hot water cylinder.

A specialist cleaning company were hired by the customers, and then they paid a local company to replace the tank and cylinder. The reason I know this is because I overheard a plumber in the merchants explaining the job he had that day, I smiled as I left, thinking...

"I am, and always have been, a heating engineer, not a plumber"

Thankfully.

EPILOGUE
Are you wanting more?

It has taken me many months to write this book, and there maybe a few more in the 'pipeline' (excuse the pun).

Adventures of me as an apprentice at college, this was of similar japes, and mishaps, but under the control of college lecturers.

Also, my life growing up in my old shire of Witney. Raleigh 1-2-3, skin heads, borstal, pond plunge, near fatal car crash, and many more.

Certain aspects of life were taking over, as I wrote this book, my mum has been in and out of hospital for over two years with different health issues, she had the diagnosis of stage 4 lung cancer (terminal) April 2023, with not years, but months to live at the ripe old age of 79.

July 17th 2023 - To which she finally passed away at 2am, in her sleep, in her own bed, in her bungalow, and in no pain, as the big 'C' hadn't had chance to take hold of our little mum... F*CK YOU CANCER!

My personal thanks go to Lou and Amy, for your dedication, and helping our mum find her resting place with you being there.

To my sisters for being there, when I wasn't.

Rest in Peace Mummy, love from Carole, Lynne & Stephen xxx

The loss of my dearest of friends Rob in December 2021, no idea why he did it, none of us did. I'm not religious, but I know that we'll meet in the next life, part of me went when you did, I love you mate, I miss you, I always will.

Life throws a lot of different objects in our way as we age, how we deal with them is down to who we are as individuals, along with help from those around us, mainly friends and family. However, never forget, we are individuals…amazing individuals at that.

I have met so many people in my life, too many to mention, who are wonderful, fantastic people.

Some were from BG…

Martin Bartlett, you are **one** of them.

Thanks,

Spike.

Printed in Great Britain
by Amazon

26930989R00078